356-10
26

THE JEWISH SANCTUARY

INSTITUTE OF RELIGIOUS ICONOGRAPHY
STATE UNIVERSITY GRONINGEN

ICONOGRAPHY OF RELIGIONS

EDITED BY

TH. P. VAN BAAREN, L. P. VAN DEN BOSCH, L. LEERTOUWER, F. LEEMHUIS,
H. TE VELDE, H. WITTE, and H. BUNING (*Secretary*)

SECTION XXIII: JUDAISM

FASCICLE ONE

LEIDEN
E. J. BRILL
1983

THE JEWISH SANCTUARY

BY

JOSEPH GUTMANN

Professor of Art History, Wayne State University, Detroit, Michigan

With 48 plates

LEIDEN

E. J. BRILL

1983

The United Library
Garrett-Evangelical/Seabury-Western Seminaries
Evanston, IL 60201

ISBN   90 04 06893 7

Copyright 1983 by E. J. Brill, Leiden, The Netherlands

All rights reserved. No part of this book may be reproduced or translated in any form, by print, photoprint, microfilm, microfiche or any other means without written permission from the publisher

PRINTED IN THE NETHERLANDS

The United Library
Garrett-Evangelical/Seabury-Western Seminaries
Evanston, IL 60201

NK 1672
.G87
GESW

CONTENTS

ACKNOWLEDGEMENTS

Most of the photographs reproduced in this fascicle come from the late Prof. Franz Landsberger, Director of the Hebrew Union College Museum, who graciously bequeathed his valuable collection of photographs to me.

My sincere thanks to Mr. Alfred Rubens for his gracious help in making photographs of objects in his collection available and to Ms. J. Montagu, Head of the photographic collection of the Warburg Institute for her assistance. A special debt is due to Prof. Stanley F. Chyet for reading the manuscript and making many helpful suggestions for its improvement.

I also wish to acknowledge the help of Alice Greenwald, Nancy Berman and Shalom Sabar of the Hebrew Union College Skirball Museum, Grace Grossman of the Maurice Spertus Museum of Judaica, Chaya Benjamin and Richard Cohen of the Israel Museum, Dr. Katia Guth-Dreyfus of the Jüdisches Museum der Schweiz and Judith Maslin.

Grateful acknowledgement for permission to reproduce photographs in their possession is made to the authorities concerned. Sources of photographs are indicated in the explanations to the plates.

SELECTED BIBLIOGRAPHY

BARASH, D., "Tik of the Sefer Torah," *Sinai*, 15 (1952), 228-236 (Hebrew).

BAŽANTOVA, N., "Byzantinische Traditionen in der synagogalen Textilkunst des 18. Jhs.?" *Byzantinoslavica*, 38 (1977), 39-40.

BEMPORAD, D. L., "Arte ceremoniale ebraica in Italia," *Commentari*, 25 (1974), 258-270.

BIALER, Y. L., *Jewish Life in Art and Tradition. Based on the Collection of the Sir Isaac and Lady Edith Wolfson Museum*, Hechal Shlomo, Jerusalem. New York, 1976.

BLUMENKRANZ, B., ed., *Art et archéologie des juifs en France médiévale*. Toulouse, 1980.

BÖCHER, O., "Die alte Synagoge zu Worms," in *Festschrift zur Wiedereinweihung der alten Synagoge zu Worms*, ed. by E. Roth, Frankfurt/Main, 1961, 11-154.

BODENSCHATZ, J. C. G., *Kirchliche Verfassung der heutigen Juden sonderlich derer in Deutschland*. Erlang, 1748.

BRILLING, B., "Geschichte des jüdischen Goldschmiedegewerbes in Schlesien," *Hamburger Mittel- und Ostdeutsche Forschungen*, 6 (1967), 163-221.

——, "Zur Geschichte des jüdischen Goldschmiedegewerbes in Prag," *Zeitschrift für die Geschichte der Juden*, 5 (1968), 21-26.

——, "Zur Geschichte des jüdischen Goldschmiedegewerbes in Mähren (1550-1800)," *Zeitschrift für die Geschichte der Juden*, 6 (1969), 137-146.

BUSINK, T., *Der Tempel von Jerusalem von Salomo bis Herodes*. Leiden, 1970, 1980, 2 vols.

CHILL, A., *The Minhagim: The Customs and Ceremonies of Judaism, Their Origins and Rationale*. New York, 1980[2].

CASSUTO, U., "Construzione rituali ebraiche nell'alto medioevo," *Settimane di studio del centro italiano di studi sull'alto medioevo*, XXVI, Spoleto, 1980, 1017-1057.

ČERMÁKOVÁ, J., "The Synagogue Textiles," *Judaica Bohemiae*, 16 (1980), 54-59.

CHRISTIANI, F. A., *Der Juden Glaube und Aberglaube*. Leipzig, 1705.

CHRISTIANI, M. W., *Kurtze Beschreibung einer wohleingerichteten Synagog*. Regenspurg, 1723.

COHEN, Y., "Torah Breastplates from Augsburg in the Israel Museum," *Israel Museum News*, 14 (1978), 75-85.

CUSIN, S. G., *Art in the Jewish Tradition*. Milan, 1963.

DAVIDOVITCH, D., "A Rare Parokhet for the Circumcision Ceremony," *Museum Haaretz Yearbook*, 15-16 (1974), 112-118.

DETROIT INSTITUTE OF ARTS, *Exhibition of Jewish Ceremonial Art*. Detroit, 1951.

DOLEZELOVÁ, J., "Binders and Festive Covers from the Collection of the State Jewish Museum in Prague," *Judaica Bohemiae*, 10 (1974), 91-104.

——, "Torah Binders from Four Centuries at the State Jewish Museum in Prague," *Judaica Bohemiae*, 9 (1973), 55-71.

DOTHAN, A., "On the History of the Ancient Synagogue in Aleppo," *Sefunot*, 1 (1956), 25-61 (Hebrew).

EHRLICH, L. E., *Die Kultsymbolik im Alten Testament und im nachbiblischen Judentum*. Stuttgart, 1959.

EISENSTEIN, J. D., *Ozar Dinim u-Minhagim*. Tel-Aviv, 1970 (Hebrew).

FRANKEL, G., "Little Known Handicrafts of Polish Jews in the Nineteenth and Twentieth Centuries," *Journal of Jewish Art*, 2 (1975), 42-49.

FREEHOF, S. B., *Reform Jewish Practice and its Rabbinic Background*. Cincinnati, 1944, 1952, 2 vols.

GOITEIN, S. D., "The Synagogue Building and its Furnishings according to the Records of the Cairo Geniza," *Eretz-Israel*, 7 (1964), 94-95 (Hebrew).

GOLDBERG, A. M., "Der siebenarmige Leuchter, zur Entstehung eines jüdischen Bekenntnissymbols," *Zeitschrift der Deutschen Morgenländischen Gesellschaft*, 117 (1967), 232-246.

GRIMWADE, A. G., *Anglo-Jewish Silver*. London, 1955.

GROSSMAN, C., "Womanly Arts: A Study of Italian Torah Binders in the New York Jewish Museum Collection," *Journal of Jewish Art*, 7 (1980), 35-43.

GUTMANN, J., ed., *The Temple of Solomon: Archaeological Fact and Medieval Tradition in Christian, Islamic and Jewish Art*. Missoula, 1976.

——, ed., *Ancient Synagogues: The State of Research*. Chico, 1981.

——, ed., *The Synagogue: Studies in Origins, Archaeology and Architecture*. New York, 1975.
——, ed., *Beauty in Holiness: Studies in Jewish Customs and Ceremonial Art*. New York, 1970.
——, *Jewish Ceremonial Art*. New York-London, 1968[2].
——, "Torah Ornaments, Priestly Vestments, and the King James Bible," *Beauty in Holiness*, ed. Gutmann, 122-124.
——, "How Traditional are Our Traditions?" *Beauty in Holiness*, ed. Gutmann, 417-419.
——, "A Note on the Temple Menorah," *No Graven Images: Studies in Art and the Hebrew Bible*, ed. Gutmann, New York, 1971, 36-38.
HAGAN, R., D. DAVIDOVITCH, R. BUSCH, *Tora Wimpel: Zeugnisse jüdischer Volkskunst aus dem Braunschweigischen Landesmuseum*. Braunschweig, 1978.
HALLO, R., *Jüdische Kunst aus Hessen und Nassau*. Berlin, 1933.
——, *Jüdische Volkskunst in Hessen*. Kassel, 1928.
HEBREW UNION COLLEGE SKIRBALL MUSEUM. *A Walk Through the Past*, ed. by N. Berman. Los Angeles, 1974.
HERBENOVÁ, O., "Synagogenvorhänge des 17. Jahrhunderts aus Böhmen und Mähren," *Waffen- und Kostümkunde*, 10 (1968), 107-126.
HINTZE, E., *Katalog der ... Ausstellung. Das Judentum in der Geschichte Schlesiens*. Breslau, 1929.
HISTORICA HEBRAICA, *Ausstellungs-Katalog des Staatlichen Jüdischen Museums Prag in Zusammenarbeit mit der Jüdischen Gemeinde zu Berlin*, ed. by I. Pruschnowski. Berlin, 1965.
HISTORISCHES MUSEUM FRANKFURT AM MAIN, *Synagoga. Jüdische Altertümer, Handschriften und Kultgeräte*. Frankfurt/Main, 1961.
HRÁSKÝ, J., "La corporation juive d'orfèvrerie à Prague," *Judaica Bohemiae*, 2 (1966), 19-40.
——, "Die Kennzeichnung von Edelmetallen," *Judaica Bohemiae*, 2 (1966), 97-106.
JEWISH ART TREASURES IN VENICE, ed. by G. Reinisch Sullam. New York, n.d.
JEWISH ART TREASURES FROM PRAGUE. *The State Jewish Museum in Prague and its Collection. Catalog of Exhibition at Whitworth Art Gollery*, ed. by C. R. Dodwell. London-Manchester, 1980.
JEWISH COMMUNITY OF ROME, *Permanent Exhibition Catalogue*. Rome, n.d.
JEWISH MUSEUM LONDON, *Catalogue of the Permanent and Loan Collections of the Jewish Museum London*, ed. by R. D. Barnett. London, 1974.
JEWISH MUSEUM NEW YORK, *Danzig 1939: Treasures of a Destroyed Community*, ed. by V. Mann and J. Gutmann. New York-Detroit, 1980.
——, *Fabric of Jewish Life. Textiles from the Jewish Museum Collection*, ed. by B. Kirschenblatt-Gimblett and C. Grossman. New York, 1977.
JEWISH HISTORICAL MUSEUM AMSTERDAM, *Joods Historisch Museum*, ed. by J. C. E. Belinfante. Haarlem, 1978.
JUDAICA: *Die Sammlung Berger*, ed. by M. Berger, W. Häusler, E. Lessing. Munich, 1979.
KANOF, A., *Jewish Ceremonial Art and Religious Observance*. New York, 1970.
KATZ, K., P. P. KAHANE, M. BROSHI, *From the Beginning. Archaeology and Art in the Israel Museum Jerusalem*. London, 1968.
KAYSER, S. S. and G. SCHOENBERGER, *Jewish Ceremonial Art*. Philadelphia, 1959[2].
KIRCHNER, P. C., *Jüdisches Ceremoniel*. Nürnberg, 1726.
KLAGSBALD, V., "L'art cultuel juif en Maroc," *Revue des études juives*, 134 (1975), 142-151.
KRAUSS, S., "The Jewish Rite of Covering the Head," *Beauty in Holiness*, ed. Gutmann, 420-467.
——, *Synagogale Altertümer*. Berlin-Vienna, 1922.
KRAUTHEIMER, R., *Mittelalterliche Synagogen*. Berlin, 1927.
KRÜGER, R., *Die Kunst der Synagoge. Eine Einführung in die Probleme von Kunst und Kult des Judentums*. Leipzig, 1966.
KYBALOVÁ, L., "Die ältesten Thoramäntel aus der Textiliensammlung des Staatlichen Jüdischen Museums in Prag (1592-1750)," *Judaica Bohemiae*, 9 (1973), 23-42.
——, "Thoramäntel aus der Textiliensammlung des Staatlichen Jüdischen Museums in Prag (1750-1800)," *Judaica Bohemiae*, 10 (1974), 69-90.
LANDESMUSEUM MÜNSTER, *Jüdisches Jahr, Jüdischer Brauch, Exhibition Catalog*. Münster, 1972.
LANDSBERGER, F., "Old-Time Torah Curtains," *Beauty in Holiness*, ed. Gutmann, 125-163.
——, "The Origin of European Torah Decorations", *Beauty in Holiness*, ed. Gutmann, 87-105.
——, "A German Torah Ornamentation," *Beauty in Holiness*, ed. Gutmann, 106-121.
——, "Old Hanukkah Lamps," *Beauty in Holiness*, ed. Gutmann, 290-309.
LAZAR, H., "Jonah, the Tower, and the Lions: An Eighteenth-Century Italian Silver Book Binding," *Journal of Jewish Art*, 3/4 (1977), 58-73.
LEVINSON, P. N., *Kultsymbolik im Alten Testament und im nachbiblischen Judentum*. Stuttgart, 1972 (Illustrations to the work by EHRLICH).

LLOMPART, G., "La fecha y circunstancias del arribo de los 'rimmonim' de la catedral de Mallorca," *Sefarad*, 30 (1970), 48-51.

LOEB-LAROCQUE, L., "Ewig-Licht Ampel (jüdisch)," *Reallexikon zur deutschen Kunstgeschichte*, VI (1973), 639-648.

MATTS, A., *Reasons for Jewish Customs and Traditions*. New York, 1968.

MAURICE SPERTUS MUSEUM OF JUDAICA, CHICAGO, *An Illustrated Catalog of Selected Objects*, ed. by A. Feldman, and G. C. Grossman, Chicago, 1974.

MELLINKOFF, R., "The Round-Topped Tablets of the Law: Sacred Symbol and Emblem of Evil," *Journal of Jewish Art*, 1 (1974), 28-43.

MEYERS, C. L., *The Tabernacle Menorah*. Missoula, 1976.

MISHKAN LE'OMANUT. *Museum of Art, Ein Harod*, ed. by Z. Efron. Ein Harod, 1970.

MITTEILUNGEN DER GESELLSCHAFT ZUR ERFORSCHUNG JÜDISCHE KUNSTDENKMÄLER ZU FRANKFURT AM MAIN, I-X. Düsseldorf—Frankfurt/Main, 1900-1927.

MOSES, E., *Jüdische Kult- und Kunstdenkmäler. Aus der Geschichte der Juden im Rheinland*. Düsseldorf, 1931.

MUNELES, O., *Prague Ghetto in the Renaissance Period*. Prague, 1965.

NAHON, U., *Holy Arks and Ritual Appurtenances from Italy in Israel*. Tel-Aviv, 1970 (Hebrew and English).

PIATELLI, A. A., "Un arazzo veneziano del XVII secolo," *La Rassegna Mensile di Israel*, 36 (1970), 315-322.

PICART, B., *The Ceremonies and Religious Customs of the Various Nations of the Known World*. London, 1733.

POSEN, I., "Die Mainzer Thoraschrein Vorhänge," *Notizblatt der Gesellschaft zur Erforschung jüdischer Kunstdenkmäler*, 29 (1932), 2-12.

RABINOWITZ, L. I., "Tefillin," *Encyclopaedia Judaica* (Jerusalem, 1971), XV, 898-914.

ROSENAN, N., *L'année juive.Vue à travers l'exposition du Musée Juif de Suisse à Bâle*. Zurich, 1976.

ROSENBAUM, J. W., *Myer Myers, Goldsmith*, 1723-1795. Philadelphia, 1954.

ROTH, C., ed., *Jewish Art. An Illustrated History*. New York, Toronto, London, 1961.

ROYAL ALBERT HALL LONDON, *Catalogue of Anglo-Jewish Historical Exhibition*, 1887. London, 1887.

RUBENS, A., *A Jewish Iconography*. London, 1981, revised edition.

SCHOENBERGER, G., "The Ritual Silver Made by Myer Myers," *Beauty in Holiness*, ed. Gutmann, 66-78.

——, "Der Frankfurter Goldschmied Johann Mathias Sandrart (geboren: Johann Matthaeus Sandrat), 1683-1750," *Schriften des Historischen Museums Frankfurt am Main*, 12 (1966), 143-170.

SCHOLEM, G., "Magen David," *Encyclopaedia Judaica* (Jerusalem, 1971), XI, 687-697.

SHACHAR, I., *Osef Feuchtwanger: Masoret veOmanut Yehudit*. Jerusalem, 1971 (Hebrew).

SMITH, M., "The Image of God: Notes on the Hellenization of Judaism, with Especial Reference to Goodenough's Work on Jewish Symbols," *Bulletin of the John Rylands Library*, 40 (1958), 473-512.

SPERBER, D., "The History of the Menorah," *The Journal of Jewish Studies*, 16 (1965), 135-159.

STÄDTISCHES MUSEUM GÖTTINGEN. *700 Jahre Juden in Südniedersachsen. Geschichte und religiöses Leben*. Göttingen, 1973.

STADTMUSEUM KÖLN, *Monumenta Judaica. 2000 Jahre Geschichte und Kultur am Rhein, Katalog*, ed. K. Schilling. Cologne, 1964.

STEMBERGER, G., *Das klassische Judentum: Kultur und Geschichte der rabbinischen Zeit*. Munich, 1979.

STONE, J., "English Silver Rimmonim and their Makers," *Quest*, 1 (1965), 23-29.

STRAUSS, H., "Menorah," *Encyclopaedia Judaica* (1971), XI, 1355-1370.

VOLAVKOVÁ, H., *The Synagogue Treasures of Bohemia and Moravia*. Prague, 1949.

WENDEL, C., *Der Thoraschrein im Altertum*. Halle, 1950.

WERNER, A., "Modern Ritual Art," *Beauty in Holiness*, ed. Gutmann, 79-84.

YADIN, Y., *Tefillin from Qumran*. Jerusalem, 1969.

YARDEN, L., *The Tree of Light: A Study of the Menorah*. Ithaca, 1971.

ZIMMELS, H. J., *Ashkenazim and Sephardim. Their Relations, Differences, and Problems as Reflected in the Rabbinical Responsa*. London, 1958.

INTRODUCTION

The synagogue has been the most important Jewish institution for the last two thousand years. Its functions are clearly spelled out in the very names it bears—*bet ha-tefillah* (house of prayer), *bet ha-midrash* (house of learning or study) and *bet ha-kenesset* (house of assembly). It has been rightly called the spiritual mother of the church and the mosque. For a thousand years prior to the synagogue, the Temple of Jerusalem served Judaism as its central cultic shrine. Built by King Solomon in the tenth century B.C.E. (I Kings 6 ff.), destroyed in 586 B.C.E., and rebuilt on a much smaller scale by the returning exiles from Babylonia in the sixth century B.C.E. (Ezra 3 ff.), the Temple was enlarged by King Herod in the first century B.C.E. and finally destroyed by the Romans in 70 C.E.[1] The prime goal of the Temple as a cultic shrine was to insure fertility of the land in an essentially agrarian economy. This was achieved by the daily sacrificial offerings which intermediary priests presented Yahweh on the Temple altar. The cultic rites and sacrifices were regulated by the Pentateuch, especially the Book of Leviticus. The Temple of Jerusalem was not rebuilt after its destruction in the first century, although an abortive attempt to rebuild it was made by the Emperor Julian in the fourth century C.E. By then the Temple had long been superseded by a novel institution known as the synagogue.

There is no consensus of agreement among scholars as to why, when and where the synagogal institution began. Traditional Jews claim a Mosaic origin for the synagogue, but many scholars opt for a Babylonian origin in the sixth century B.C.E. on the grounds that, in the absence of a Temple, the exiled Jews needed an institution like the synagogue and on the basis of a statement by the tenth-century Gaon of Pumbedita, Sherira ben Ḥanina, that when Israel was exiled to Babylonia King Jehoiachin built a synagogue in Nehardea, using for its foundation earth and stones brought from the ruins of the Temple in Jerusalem. Other scholars claim that the synagogue must have emerged during the "Deuteronomic Reformation" in Judah during the seventh century B.C.E. when the destruction of local shrines (*bamot*) left the rural countryside with a void which only a meeting place like the synagogue could have filled. Some scholars feel that the synagogue's origins must be sought in third-century Egypt since we find houses of prayer (*proseuchai*) mentioned there. These houses of prayer are automatically equated by many scholars with the synagogue. The theories of a Babylonian, Judean or Egyptian origin for the synagogue rest largely on *argumenta ex silentio* as there is no secure archaeological evidence of the synagogue's existence before the third century C.E. "Factual" proof for the existence of the synagogue is largely grounded in semantic arguments. Expressions like *mikdash meʿat*, *bet ha-am*, *moʿadei-el* are ripped from their biblical moorings and given a meaning which they actually acquired only at a later period. Similarly, the "houses of

---

[1] Cf. J. Gutmann, ed. *The Temple of Solomon: Archaeological Fact and Medieval Tradition in Christian, Islamic and Jewish Art* (Missoula, 1976), and T. Busink, *Der Tempel von Jerusalem von Salomo bis Herodes* (Leiden, 1970, 1980), 2 vols.

prayer'' (*proseuchai*) of Egypt need not have been synagogues. Prayers might have been uttered in connection with cultic practices, to affirm loyalty to reigning princes, or as part of a mystery religion. Precisely what the *proseuchai* were has never been definitely ascertained.

The emergence of the synagogue is probably connected with the Hasmonaean Revolution in second-century B.C.E. Judea and the rise of a new scholar class known as the Pharisees. The Judaism the Pharisees forged was a radical restructuring of Pentateuchalism. Using the Pentateuch as a proof text they created a novel two-fold legal system known as the Written and Oral Law and a new institution known as the synagogue. The Written Law referred to the writings which form the Hebrew Bible and the Oral Law to the pronouncements and legislation of the rabbis; both the Written and the Oral Law had ostensibly been handed to Moses at Sinai. Synagogues were decentralized meeting places for the recitation and interpretation of the Torah (the pentateuchal scroll) and the Prophets. Gradually, after the destruction of the Temple in 70 C.E., synagogal prayers and ceremonial practices, in addition to Torah and Prophetic readings, took the place of the lapsed sacrifices; the heirs of the Pharisees (now called rabbis) replaced the priests.

Loss of the Jerusalem Temple could, however, not easily be eradicated from Jewish memory. After all, it had been God's house. Why had it been destroyed? Why had God abandoned it? The rabbis tried to demonstrate that God had had no alternative, but had not abandoned Israel. His wrath was kindled against Israel's shortcomings and against the untrustworthy guardians (= priests) of His Temple, against those who had violated God's trust by making His place unworthy for worship. God had, therefore, decided to destroy His Temple. The rabbis tried to show that God would build a more splendid Temple in the messianic future and that the destroyed Second Temple had never measured up to the sanctity of the First and was not worthy of being rebuilt. In the meantime, the synagogue would be a *mikdash me'at* (a lesser or minor sanctuary), a surrogate or temporary substitute for the future Temple. To further underscore the important role of the synagogue, the worshippers were instructed to face, in their prayers, towards the former Temple in Jerusalem. Synagogal buildings, therefore, were frequently oriented towards Jerusalem or at any rate towards the East. Since the synagogue had become a surrogate Temple, it was legitimate to practice in it what formerly had been the exclusive prerogatives of the Jerusalem Temple. Thus not only were Torah readings and prayers and study equated with the offering of sacrifices in the Temple, but the Temple-centered festivals were kept in transmuted form and the synagogal liturgy was patterned on the Temple's thrice daily mode of worship. In the synagogue, the individual Jew could affirm his loyalty to the two-fold Pharisaic law with the guarantee that the observance of the new laws (*halakhot*) would bring about salvation of the soul after death and bodily resurrection in the messianic age. Thus instead of fertility of the land which the priestly Temple cult assured, the Pharisaic religion promised salvation and resurrection for each individual Jew.

Although the existence of the synagogue is well attested to by such first century C.E. sources as Josephus and the New Testament, the synagogal buildings mentioned are not liable to identification since they are probably indistinguishable from domestic architecture until the third century C.E. The excavated synagogues in Palestine and the Diaspora reveal such a rich diversity of architectural forms, styles, and orientation that they challenge the accepted scholarly view of a rigid "normative rabbinic Judaism" prevailing during this period. Rather the buildings point to distinct local and regional Jewish traditions both in the Diaspora and in Palestine. The architecture of the buildings, which will not be discussed,[2] closely follows the contemporary structural and stylistic forms. Thus in the Byzantine period, the classical basilica frequently served as a model for the synagogue, just as the Romanesque and Gothic styles were later adapted for synagogal use in Europe. These adaptations were, of course, modified to conform to the requirements of Jewish worship and in keeping with certain restraints imposed by the society in which the Jewish minority lived. To be sure, such rabbis as Judah Assad in the nineteenth century counseled his Orthodox followers not to change the prevailing synagogue architectural styles, and denounced Reform Judaism's attempt to use contemporary synagogue architecture "as a sin of those who pant after the spirit of the times to destroy our ancient customs to imitate other religions." By and large, however, most rabbis paid little heed to architectural styles and would have agreed with the eighteenth-century Prague rabbi, Ezekiel Landau, who felt that the shape and design of a synagogue are of little consequence.[3]

The synagogue has been variously designated throughout the ages. Originally it was called *synagōgē* (synagogue) or its Hebrew equivalent *bet ha-kenesset* or Aramaic *bei khenishta*. In medieval Europe it was called *schola* (or *scola*; later *scuola* in Italy, *Schule* in Germany and *Shul* in Poland). *Mikdash me'at* is also a common designation for the synagogue, and in the nineteenth century Reform synagogues were called Temples.

From the third to the seventh century C.E. our information about synagogues comes mainly from excavations of Palestinian synagogues and widely scattered synagogues in Europe and North Africa. The synagogues that existed in such great Jewish centers of learning as Nehardea, Sura, Maḥuza and Pumbedita in the Parthian and Sasanian empires have not been found, although they are mentioned in the Babylonian Talmud. The synagogue of Dura-Europos in third-century Syria with its important cycle of biblical illustrations has sometimes been cited as a Babylonian synagogue, yet close examination reveals that the style of the paintings is Syro-Palestinian and the theology behind the mural program is drawn from the Judaism of the same region and has minimal relationship to Babylonian Judaism.[4]

Even the early Jewish involvement in the Islamic civilizations has left us with little substantive information about synagogues. The development of the synagogue and its ceremonial appurtenances really stems from the Middle Ages: the earliest surviving medieval synagogue may be the recently discovered building of Rouen, France, dating from around 1100.[5]

Extant synagogue objects, although we know from rabbinic texts that they existed earlier, date only from the fifteenth century. Our study of the synagogal furnishings then

---

[2] On synagogue origins and on the architecture of the early synagogue, cf. J. Gutmann, ed., *Ancient Synagogues: The State of Research* (Chico, 1981), and J. Gutmann, ed., *The Synagogue: Studies in Origins, Archaeology and Architecture* (New York, 1975).

[3] Cf. S. Freehof, *Reform Jewish Practice*, II (Cincinnati, 1952), 11ff.

[4] Cf. J. Gutmann, ed., *The Dura-Europos Synagogue: A Re-evaluation* (Missoula, 1973).

[5] Cf. B. Blumenkranz, ed., *Art et archéologie des juifs en France médiévale* (Toulouse, 1980).

stems primarily from the Jewish involvement in the Christian and Islamic civilizations of various countries.

The most important object in the synagogue is the pentateuchal scroll (*Sefer Torah*). The *Sefer Torah*, unlike all the other appurtenances used in the synagogue, possesses *kedushah* (holiness). The other objects have no holy, transcendental value and might even be deemed expendable in times of stress or catastrophe. A Torah is so holy that it cannot be touched by human hands. When a scroll is beyond repair or worn out, it is hidden away (in a *genizah*—a special chamber or area in the synagogue), or, as is the custom in Israel, properly buried in a cemetery. Traditional Jews consider the Torah the word of God; pious worshippers rise out of respect for the holy Torah when it is taken from and returned to the Ark. "Immediately," (i.e., after the bringing the Torah to the reading desk), we are informed, the cantor or reader of the Torah "rolls the scroll of the Torah to three columns and lifts it up and shows its actual writing to the people standing on his right and on his left; and he turns it forward and backward because it is a commandment for all men and women to see the script and bow down" (*Soferim* 14:4) (Plate I). In Italy a silver bar known as a *sharbit* is often placed on the Torah staves to make certain that the Torah is spread to the prescribed three columns. It also serves as an adornment to the Torah when the scroll is undressed and raised aloft. When the Torah is taken in procession from the Torah ark to the platform (*bimah*), it should always be carried on the right arm (Isserles, *Oraḥ Ḥayyim* 134:2) and the congregants reach out to kiss it as a sign of love and respect. The Torah is read four times a week—on Monday and Thursday mornings and on Saturday mornings and afternoons, as well as on holidays and fastdays. A quorum (*minyan*) of ten men must be present. Seven men are called up to the reading of the Torah on Saturday mornings, three on Monday, Thursday and Saturday afternoons. Originally, those called up (*aliyah*) would also read their prescribed portions; now it is generally the custom for the cantor (*ḥazzan*) to recite the entire section. The first two readers must be a *kohen* (one who traces his lineage back to the *kohanim*, or priests of the Temple) and a Levi (one who traces his lineage back to the Temple Levites); the rest are Israelites or ordinary Jews. The traditional reason given for this order is based on Deuteronomy 31:9: "Moses wrote down the Teaching (*Torah*) and gave it to the priests, sons of Levi, who carried the Ark of the Covenant, and to the elders of Israel." The final ritual before returning the Torah to the ark is the *hagbahah* and *gelilah*.

After the prescribed number of men have read their portions, two additional men are called up—one lifts the Torah from the platform (*hagbahah*), while the other rolls and ties the Torah scroll (*gelilah*). According to the Babylonian Talmud (*Megillah* 32a), the person who rolls the Scroll together should do so from the outside (i.e., the parchment with the script facing the person holding it) and tie it together from the inside, while the one who raised the Torah remains seated holding it. The annual readings of the Torah are divided into 54 *sidrot* (pericopes) according to the now accepted divisions instituted by the Babylonian Talmud. The Palestinian rabbis had divided the Torah readings in keeping with a triennial cycle.[6] Specially trained devout professional scribes (*soferim*) copy the text of the Torah, a task which usually takes about nine months (Plate IIa). Only the inner sides of *kasher* (ritually slaughtered) animals are now generally used for parchment

---

[6] Cf. M. Klein, "Four Notes on the Triennial Cycle," *Journal of Jewish Studies*, 32 (1981), 65-73.

(*klaf*). In Ashkenazi countries (Franco-German and East European Jewries) a feather quill is used as the writing implement; in Sephardi (Spanish-Portuguese and Islamic Jewries) the calamus (reed pen) is preferred.The scribe is not allowed to write even a single word from memory; he must pronounce every word before copying it from a correct text. If the scribe makes more than four mistakes in a column, that whole parchment section must be discarded and written again.

Decorative crownlets (*taggin*) are added to the tops of thirteen of the twenty-two Hebrew letters. Seven letters (ץ ז) (ש ע ט נ ז ג צ) require a three crown stroke (*tag*) to the left of the letter; six (ב ד ק ח י ה) require one stroke (*tag*) (Plate IIb). Six letters are written particularly small—for example the *alef* in the first word of Leviticus (*vayikra*). Eleven letters are written very large, such as the *bet* in the opening word of the Torah, *bereshit*. The poetic verses of *shirat hayam* (Exodus 15:1-18) are arranged in thirty lines so as to resemble bricks in a wall (Babylonian Talmud, *Shabbat* 103b). The poetic verses of the section *ha'azinu* (Deuteronomy 31:1-43) are placed in seventy double rows—a practice to which Rabbi Meir of Rothenburg strongly objected (*Responsa* II, 150).

The Torah is written without vowels or punctuation marks and its parchment pages are sewn together with threads of sinew (*gidin*) from a *kosher* animal. Two finger's width must be left between the columns of writing; 60 lines of writing to a page, but not less than 48. At the top, the scribe must leave a space of three finger's width; at the bottom he must leave four finger's width. As can be seen in the fourth-century Jewish gold-leaf glasses found in Jewish catacombs of Rome, single scrolls of individual books of the Torah were apparently used (cf. Babylonian Talmud, *Gittin* 60a).

To prevent the scrolls from being mutilated as they lay piled one atop another in the chest, an *umbilicus* (*amud* = rod, pillar) was used (Plates IIIa-b). When the Torah (all five books) became one scroll, it was thought advisable to use two rods or rollers (although there are examples from the Middle Ages where only one roller is used). These rods or rollers are sewn to the ends of the parchment so that the scroll can be lifted from the chest without being touched. The Babylonian Talmud (*Baba Batra* 14a) further mentions that other kinds of scrolls are rolled from end to end, but supplied with a pillar (*amud*) at each side; the Scroll of the Law is rolled towards its middle. The pillars or rollers (called *amudim* and later *atzei ḥayyim*—the reference in Proverbs 3:18 "a *tree of life* is she to all who lay hold of her" is taken to refer to the Torah) are usually made of wood, although silver rollers and rollers covered with silver, especially from seventeenth-eighteenth century Holland, were also used.[7]

The Torah is likened to a princess and a bride, hence has been regally adorned since earliest times. The adornments of the Torah consist of such embroidered textiles as binders and mantles, known as *bigdei kodesh*, and silver decorations known as *klei kodesh*—crowns, headpieces, cases, pointers and plates (Plate IIb). The association of the Torah with royalty is well established in Jewish literary sources; the link with the Jerusalem Temple priesthood so often made in scholarly religious texts is not warranted. The adornments of the Torah are not analogous to the vestments worn by Aaron, the priest. Such

---

[7] F. Landsberger, "The Origin of European Torah Decorations," in J. Gutmann, ed., *Beauty in Holiness* (New York, 1970), 87ff.

an assumption, if true, would imply an unbroken and ancient tradition for the employ-
ment of these implements in both the Jerusalem Temple and the synagogue. Thus the
Torah plate or shield is commonly called a *hoshen*, corresponding to the so-called "breastpiece" (Exodus 28:4) or, less frequently, the *tzitz*, "the frontlet" of pure gold (Exodus
28:36), both worn by Aaron, the priest, in the Temple. Such associations are never made
in rabbinic literature, however, and only a few isolated Torah shields in the nineteenth
century are so identified. Similarly, the Torah headpieces (now usually referred to as
rimmonim) are frequently derived from the "golden bell and pomegranate (*rimmon*) all
around the hem of Aaron's robe" (Exodus 28:34), yet no warrant for such an association is
found in rabbinic sources. Moreover, the words *hoshen mishpat* (Exodus 28:15) denote
the oracular pouch worn by Aaron; the pouch was made of cloth and not metal, as we
find in the Torah shield.

The word breastplate, a common designation for the Torah shield in many textbooks,
apparently became part of the English language through the King James Bible trans-
lation of 1611. The word *hoshen* is here rendered as breastplate, and it is most likely that
this is the source for the assumed analogy between Torah decorations and priestly vestments. The twelve tribal stones (Exodus 28:15 ff.), encountered so often on contemporary
synagogue Torah shields in conscious imitation of those of the priestly *hoshen*, have no
traditional validation as no demonstrable link exists between the Torah shield and the
priestly *hoshen*.[8]

In Islamic countries (Turkey excepted), the Torah scroll is usually kept enclosed in a
container known as *nartik* or *tik* (perhaps from the Greek, *thēkē*, box). The Torah scroll is
not removed from the container, but is always opened and read standing upright on the
reader's desk. The Babylonian Talmud (*Megillah* 26b) already mentions a *tik* (receptacle
or case) in connection with the *sefer Torah*. Such a case may be depicted in the third-
century synagogue panel at Dura-Europos next to the man reading or unveiling a Torah
scroll (Plate IV). This *tik*, however, does not resemble the *tik* found in Islamic communities
of the Middle Ages. Cairo Genizah documents dating from the eleventh and twelfth
centuries refer to wooden cases covered with silver or copper, or made entirely of copper.[9]
The cylindrical or octagonal *tik* is made of metal or wood or both; the two equal parts are
held together with a hinge at the back.

One of the oldest surviving Torah cases comes from the Samaritan community in
Damascus, Syria, and is dated 1565. Cylindrical, inlaid with copper-silver arabesque
ornaments, it undoubtedly resembled cases made for other Jewish communities. From the
small Jewish community of Keifeng in China's Honan province, some wood gilt-lacquered
cases have survived with pointed flame-shaped knobs (Plate Va). Originally wrapped in
yellow silks, these may date from the late seventeenth century. The Islamic Jewish
practice of housing the Torah scroll in a *tik* (Plates V-VI) must have been brought to
China by Levantine Jewish merchants who settled there.

An unusual Torah case, now lost, came from Aleppo, Syria, and was made in 1710 by
the Jewish artist, Joseph Laham. It was prismatic in shape, having eight silver plaques

[8] Cf. J. Gutmann, "Torah Ornaments, Priestly Vestments, and the King James Bible," *Beauty in
Holiness*, ed. J. Gutmann (New York, 1970), 122-124.
[9] Cf. S. D. Goitein, "The Synagogue Building and its Furnishings according to the Records of the
Cairo Genizah," *Eretz-Israel*, 7 (1964), 94-95 (Hebrew).

nailed to a sheathing of wood. On the plaques are engraved different scenes of the syna-gogue, its gardens, courtyard, religious artifacts, etc. (Plate Vb). Surviving cases fre-quently have either the Torah staves inside the *tik* or piercing the ceiling of the *tik*; the protruding staves are covered with *rimmonim*, sometimes in the shape of pomegranates, with bells attached to chains (Plates Va, VIa). The bulbous-shaped domes atop many *tikim* at times resemble crowns (Plate VIa). In Yemen, the Torah case is sometimes carved or inlaid. It is also wrapped in colored cloths both on the outside and inside.

In European as distinct from Islamic communities, the Torah is not enshrined in a case, but is covered with a textile garment, which is removed from the scroll to be read while lying flat in a horizontal position on the reader's desk. The Torah scroll itself is first wrapped in a binder usually referred to as *mappah* or *mitpaḥat*. (In modern Hebrew, the Torah binder is called *ḥitul*; in Germanic countries, it was called *Wimpel*, in Italy *fascia*). *Mappah* is a generic term covering all cloth—it was also employed for Torah mantles and covers for synagogue furniture. Italian Jewish communities following the Italian rite customarily recited a special public blessing every Sabbath and festival after the Torah service: "May He who blessed our mothers Sarah, Rebecca, Rachel and Leah bless every daughter of Israel who fashioned a mantle (*meʿil*) or a binder (*mitpaḥat*) in honor of the Torah ..." The Mishnah, *Kelim* 28:4, already speaks of "*mitpaḥot*, scroll wrappers, whether figures are portrayed on them or not." What the word figures refers to in this context is not certain, as no surviving Torah binders from the mishnaic period are extant.

The earliest surviving Torah binders come from sixteenth-century Italy (Plate VIIa). They are usually made of fine linen or weavepattern silk, and bear Hebrew inscriptions, sometimes the name of the donor, the occasion and the coat of arms of the Italian patri-cian family member donating the binder. The donors of these binders were usually women; such occasions as weddings or the death of a loved one prompted the gift.[10]

Binders also come from Germany. Around 1500 in South and Western Germany a significant binder custom arose. The usual linen cloth, sometimes silk, upon which the boy was circumcised, was washed, cut into three or four pieces, and stitched together into a binder which then served to bind the Torah scroll and prevent tears in the parchment. The boy's name, the date of his birth, and the standard formula "May the Lord raise him up to the study of Torah, to the *ḥuppah* (marriage canopy) and to good deeds were em-broidered—from the early eighteenth century on, painted—on what was called a *mappah* or *Wimpel* (Plates IIb, VIIb). The designation "Wimpel" is first encountered in the writings of the sixteenth-seventeenth-century Frankfurt-am-Main rabbi Joseph Yuspa Hahn. The oldest known *Wimpel*, dating from 1570, was kept in the ancient Worms synagogue, but was destroyed along with the synagogue by the Nazis. Some *Wimpeln* dating from the mid-seventeenth century have survived. The custom later spread to neighboring countries like Bohemia-Moravia and Alsace. The *Wimpel* was usually pre-sented to the synagogue in a special ceremony on the child's first visit there. It functioned as a birth certificate and sometimes contained the name of the community where it was embroidered. The Hebrew letters were often sketched by local cantors, who were also scribes, or were taken from patterns on stencils. It was a special *mitzvah* (act of religious merit) for a virgin or bride to embroider the *Wimpel*.[11]

---

[10] C. Grossman, "Womenly Arts: A Study of Italian Torah Binders in the New York Jewish Museum Collection," *Journal of Jewish Art*, 7 (1980), 35-43.
[11] Cf. fascicle XXIII/2 *The Jewish Life Cycle*.

When the Torah scroll is closed and rolled up, it is draped with a vestment, usually referred to as a *me'il—Mäntelche* or *Mäntele*—a "robe" (Exodus 28:4), but sometimes designated as a *mappah*. The Ashkenazim usually stiffen the tops of the Torah mantle and have two small round openings from which the Torah staves protrude (Plate VIII). These Torah mantles are made of a single piece of cloth looped around the Torah scroll with an aperture, garment-like or robe-like, at the bottom. Red velvet is the most common color, though green, brown, blue and white mantles are also found. On *Rosh ha-Shanah* and *Yom Kippur*, a white mantle is preferred, for the penitent worshipper is traditionally likened on these days to the ministering angels whose sinless record is as white as snow. Green is frequently used for the harvest festivals of *Sukkot* and *Shavuot*.

Sukkot—a thanksgiving observance—symbolically reminds Jews of the abundant fall harvest when they dwelt in booths covered with greenery and when they used in the Temple ritual the *lulav*, branch of the palm tree, the bough of a leafy tree and willows of the brook. In the late spring on *Shavuot*, the "Festival of the First Fruits" and the day traditionally associated with the giving of the Torah, the color green was thought to recall the grass which grew around Mount Sinai. Hence synagogues and homes are decorated with greenery. For midsummer *Tish'ah BeAv*, an annual day of mourning for the destruction of the Jerusalem Temple, a black Torah wrapping is used in some synagogues.

Matching Torah ark curtains, using the colors white, green and black, are frequently employed. Often, in gold and silver embroidery with semi-precious stones, the Torah mantles bear inscriptions recording the date, name(s) of donor(s), and occasion of the gift—whether the birth of a child, a wedding, the memorialization of a loved one, or honoring a guild or some other Jewish organization. They may feature such symbols as lions holding a crown (Plate VIII), the levitical ewer, or the blessing hands of a kohen. Some rare mantles exist which have biblical scenes embroidered on them (Plate VIIIa, IX). The oldest extant Torah mantle dates from 1592 and was donated to Prague's Maisel synagogogue by its founder, Mordecai Maisel.

The Sephardim of Holland and England generally prefer a mantle which has a soft top with two openings for the Torah staves and sometimes vertical embroidered brocade strips alternating with others not embroidered (Plate X). These Sephardi mantles open at the back and carry no extensive inscriptions; sometimes, however, they do have embroidered Jewish symbols, a short text and the Latin initials of the donor. Frequently, too, they have a large fringe encircling them one third of the way down.

In Italy, embroidered silks are the rule, although brocade is also used (Plate XXXIa). These mantles too, often have a fringe encircling the soft top about one third down like the Sephardi mantle. They open at the back and usually carry no inscriptions or symbols, but simply employ the precious fabrics and their decorations. An illustration of an Italian Torah mantle from the late fifteenth century is found in a Florentine Hebrew manuscript. It differs from mantles now in use in that it reveals a long embroidered strip which appears attached to the Torah mantle and hangs loosely from it. There is no opening for the Torah staves; they are covered by the rich fabric with its two tassels (Plate XI).

In the late Middle Ages the custom arose of adorning the Torah further by placing a plate, later a shield, in front of its textile mantle. This shield is now suspended by chains hung around the Torah staves. As more than one Torah scroll was available in large congregations and since special pericopes were read for the holidays, it became customary to place identifying plates on each scroll to indicate the occasion for which the scroll was to be used. From this practical function gradually arose the ornamental shield; the oldest extant one dates from around 1610 (Plate XIIa). The earliest reference to the Torah plate is found in a responsum of Rabbi Israel Isserlein from fifteenth-century Austria (*Terumat ha-Deshen*, Part II, par. 225): "To me it appears like a lowering of its sanctity if a rod [from which ark curtains are suspended] is converted into plates (*pahim*) [for scrolls of the Pentateuch] ... those plates that indicate the occasion on which the scrolls are to be used. Such plates are purely a matter of expediency. They are nothing but markers for preventing errors with regard to which scroll is to be read at a given time. These plates serve neither the purpose of beautifying nor that of covering the scroll."

Apparently only in the late sixteenth century does the ornamental shield make its appearance. It is called *Blech* (or *pah* = plate) by Polish and Moravian Jews, but German Jews call it *Das* (= *tas*, metal plate). At first the Torah shield was rectangular and had in its center a small rectangular opening for seven small identifying plates (*Shabbat, Rosh ha-Shanah, Yom Kippur, Sukkot, Pessah, Shavuot, Rosh Hodesh*). Gradually, from the late seventeenth century on, well-known silversmiths in such centers as Augsburg, Nuremberg and Frankfurt fashioned elaborate shields (Plates XII-XVII) often modeled after the silver shields with chains which the Christian craft and marksmen guilds used to decorate their walls at meeting houses on festive occasions or at guild funerals to adorn the bier or its black pall. Pendants with the names of donors are sometimes attached to the lower edge of the plate. Arcuated tops, cartouche-shaped sides, edges adorned with shell forms and leaves are among the varied shapes and designs in use. In imitation of title pages of Hebrew books we also find in the eighteenth century fanciful architectural shields, which have architectural ensembles with two columns supporting arches or at other times surmounted by lions supporting a crown (Plates XIV-XV).

The figures of Aaron and Moses, the menorah and the tablets of the Ten Commandments are also encountered. The *tas* is not known in Islamic communities, but is found in Italy where it appears as a small flat pendant, sometimes in the shape of a crown; it hangs by a chain from the Torah staves. These pendants simply carry the designation First, Second, Third Torah—to indicate the holidays on which they are to be used (Plate XVII, XXXIa).

To enhance the scroll's royal character further and to discourage the reader from touching the sacred text with his hands, a special pointer (now called *yad*), resembling a royal scepter, was fashioned; these pointers are most frequently made of silver or silver-gilt, but sometimes of wood, coral, ivory, etc. and are studded with semi-precious stones. When not in use, the *yad* is hung above the *tas* on an Ashkenazi Torah scroll (Plate XVIII). Among the Sephardim of Holland and England and in Italian synagogues, no chains are employed, the shapes of pointers differ, and they are kept in the ark when not in use. The early sixteenth-century convert Anthonius Margaritha records the German custom of placing on each side of the Torah scroll "a silk cloth so as not to touch the scroll with the bare hand." Moses Isserles (*Shulhan Arukh, Orah Hayyim* 154:6) from sixteenth-century Poland speaks of *etzim* (wooden pointers) made from Torah ark curtain rods to guide in reading the Torah; a century later, the Polish rabbi Abraham Abele Gombiner mentions "the custom of hanging them [*klonsaot* = pointers] on the *sefer Torah*." Pointers in the shape of a hand are referred to for the first time in a Prague archival source of 1581.

Silver pointers in the shape of a closed hand with the index finger pointed are extant no earlier than the seventeenth century; literary sources of the period refer to them as a *yad* whose index finger is used for reading the Torah (Plate XVIII).

Atop the protruding Torah staves (*atzei ḥayyim*, trees of life) were customarily placed ornaments called *rimmonim* (pomegranates), first referred to in Maimonides (*Yad, Hilkhot Sefer Torah* X:4) and in Cairo Genizah documents. Most likely these ornaments were placed on top of the staves protruding from the *tik* (Torah case). They may originally have had the shape of pomegranates, as is the case with some surviving eighteenth-nineteenth-century *rimmonim* from Islamic communities. Generally, the *rimmonim* from Islamic communities have simple spherical shapes, often resembling a fruit (Plates Vb, VIa). Although the accepted name for Torah headpieces in Islamic communities was *rimmonim*, they were also called *tzipuyei zahav* (Responsa of R. Meir of Rothenburg, *Maharam*, ed. Prag, 1608, no. 879), and *tapuḥim* (Jacob ben Asher, *Yoreh De'ah* 282.16) in European Christian communities. These golden ornaments or apples were apparently simple spherical knobs placed on the Torah staves, as can be seen in some medieval Hebrew miniatures. The knobs may not have been removable, although we read of the theft of *deux poms* (apples or knobs) from the synagogue of Perpignan, in 1463.

The oldest surviving *rimmonim*, kept in the Cathedral Treasury of Palma de Mallorca, Spain stem from Cammarata, Sicily. Dating probably from the fifteenth century, they are removable square towers with cylindrical turrets at the corners and with a cylindrical roof; pendant bells are suspended on chains from the turrets (Plate XIX). The turret or spire form with bells maintains itself in Europe with infinite variations, and some extremely fine specimens are extant from seventeenth-and eighteenth-century Europe. Many were made by Christian smiths, as Jews were excluded from the Christian craft guilds (Plate XX-XXI). Within Christendom, only in Eastern Europe were Jews allowed to form their own craft guilds, and thus only there could they fashion their own ceremonial objects. In Islamic communities, where metalsmithing was considered an inferior craft, Jews were also active in producing their own ritual objects. The names of two skilled Jewish craftsmen are known from the eighteenth century—the English craftsman Abraham de Oliveyra and the American Myer Myers—and their exquisite *rimmonim* are extant (Plates XXII-XXIII). The turret form without any curves and the more bulbous towers are generally favored in Germany, Holland, England and America. In shape modeled on church and other municipal towers, these turrets are frequently crested by a crown finial. We also find eighteenth-century *rimmonim* with pierced bulbous sections that abandon the tower shape. In Italy it is the custom to add elaborate *rimmonim* to the tops of the Torah staves and to have a crown loosely placed around their base. These three objects form a single set. We find no bells within the arcades of towers or suspended from the bulbous sections, but instead long chains with bells suspended from the lowest storey of the tower (Plate XXIV). Bells, according to a nineteenth-century rabbinic source, are to be placed on Torah ornaments, so that their tinkling will alert the congregation to rise and pay respects to the Torah (Ephraim Zalman Margolioth, *Sha'arei Efraim* 10:3). They may also have been associated with such medieval superstitious practices as warding off evil spirits. Frequently Italian *rimmonim* also feature a vase or urn with flowers as a finial. Besides the turret shape, floral, fruit and urn-shaped *rimmonim* are also found in eighteenth-nineteenth-century Italian specimens.

The Torah crowns used in Italy in conjunction with the *rimmonim* are likewise known from other Jewish communities (Plate XXIV). A crown called *atarah* is already referred to in tenth-century Gaonic sources. Hai ben Sherira, Gaon of Pumbeditha, Babylonia, states: "They make a crown (*atarah*) for the Torah, either of gold, of silver, or of myrtle, of women's ornaments, such as rings, etc. And we place them on the *sefer Torah* when it is within the case (*tik*), or upon the case on *Simhat Torah*." Special crowns of this sort were made for the holiday of *Simhat Torah* (Plate XXV). It also became customary in the Middle Ages to place such crowns on the reader of the Torah—the *hatan Bereshit* ("bride-groom of Genesis," an honorific title for the person designated to read the first portion of the Torah), and the *hatan Torah* ("bridegroom of Torah," the man honored in the reading of the final portion of the Torah). These "bridegrooms" are assigned special seats next to the Torah ark in some synagogues (Plate XXXa). The early synagogue also included a chair called *cathedra of Moses*, a seat of honor which symbolically endowed the occupant with authority—inherited from Moses—to interpret Jewish law. Kabbalistic sources likened the Torah to a bride and Israel to a bridegroom. Israel is thus annually betrothed to his bride, Torah, and both are festively adorned for their symbolic marriage. This custom was especially at home among Sephardim and is reported as early as the thirteenth century in Spain. We have little knowledge of the shape of the crowns used for these symbolic purposes. Some miniatures in medieval Spanish Haggadot of the fourteenth century appear to depict a crown on the Torah scroll. A crown (*atarah*) is mentioned in fourteenth-century Spanish sources and in an archival source from 1477 in Arles, France. The earliest surviving crowns date from the seventeenth century.

The *atarah* is now called *keter Torah* in many Western Jewish communities. Often such a crown is placed on the Torah staves directly, or *rimmonim* and crown are so fashioned as to form one unit to be mounted on the Torah staves (Plates XXVI-XXVII). These crowns were used on significant holidays only, not on Sabbath or weekdays. The closed crown made of silver or silver-gilt with precious stones is a common synagogue ap-purtenance in Western Europe and generally resembles a royal diadem (Plate XXVI, XXVIIa). Only in eighteenth- and nineteenth-century Polish crowns do we find animals and griffins or lions holding up parts of the elaborate crown structures (Plate XXVIII). The open silver or bronze or brass crowns of Italian synagogues generally resemble crowns of the Madonna (Plates XXIVa, XXIX, XXXIa). They frequently carry such Jewish symbols as a *menorah*, tablets of the Ten Commandments, etc.

The Torah scrolls were housed in a special container known as a *tevah*, later called *aron ha-kodesh* in Ashkenazi and *hekhal* in Sephardi synagogues. In the early synagogue, Torah scrolls were kept in portable Torah arks, stored probably in an adjoining room (Babylonian Talmud, *Sotah* 39b) and brought into the synagogue at the time of the ceremony or for services only. Such a portable ark may be depicted in the paintings of the Dura-Europos synagogue. The Torah niche, in a synagogue like Dura's served simply like the *kiblah* in the mosque to indicate the direction of prayer. Gradually the Torah ark became a fixed repository placed in a niche or an apse of the synagogue, as can been in synagogue mo-saics (Plate XLVIII), gold-leaf glasses (Plate III) and catacomb paintings dating from the third to sixth century. The *tevah* is often a carved double-doored book chest with gabled or arched top, usually supported by columns and a conch within the gabled or arched top (Plates III, XLVIII). The Torah scrolls are positioned horizontally as in a book chest (Plate III). Generally the orientation of prayer in synagogues was towards the east—or towards Jerusalem.

In some of the earliest synagogues, the synagogue entrance and later the Torah ark/ shrine faced toward Jerusalem. Unlike the Church's practice of a sacred direction linked with a god, with Christ, the synagogue orientation was linked with a geographic place, with Jerusalem. For Christianity the east was important since Christ was the symbolic rising sun, whose second coming was eagerly awaited from that direction. For Jews, too, the east was important, since Jerusalem was to be the site of the ultimate messianic fulfillment with the rebuilding of Solomon's Temple and the resurrection of the dead. The oldest surviving ark comes from thirteenth-century Islamic Egypt. It is simply a free-standing wooden chest in which the Torah cases were placed in an upright position. In early medieval European synagogues, the Torah ark is sometimes a permanent wall niche closed by doors with a Gothic stone gable on top. Free-standing wooden ark-chests, distinguished from ordinary chests only by their Hebrew inscriptions, are also depicted in late fourteenth-and fifteenth-century Hebrew miniatures. Some of these wooden arks from late-fifteenth century Italy have survived. In Dutch and English Sephardi synagogues are found wooden cabinets with columns along the entire eastern walls, often resembling retables in churches (Plate XXX). Eastern European synagogues included exuberant baroque ark structures with volutes, lions and fluted pilasters; sometimes they bear the inscription: "Know before whom you stand" (Babylonian Talmud, *Berakhot* 28b), and steps usually lead up to the ark in keeping with Psalm 130:1 "Out of the depths have I called You, O Lord." The placing of the tablets of the Ten Commandments above the Torah ark is unknown in early and medieval synagogues, but appears only in the seventeenth century. The talmudic sages had removed the Decalogue from the daily liturgy to confound sectarians (Babylonian Talmud, *Berakhot* 12a); later rabbis strictly forbade the use of the Decalogue in the liturgy and as synagogal decoration. In sixteenth-century Italian synagogues, the Decalogue often appears written out in the interior of wooden Torah ark doors (Plate XXXI). The round-topped tablets, now so common, appear for the first time in eleventh-century English Christian manuscripts.[12] From the eighteenth-century on some miniature silver arks made for the homes of wealthy Jews have also been preserved (Plate XXXII).

A curtain, now called *parokhet* (also *vilon* and *yeri'ah*) often hung in front of the ark, as is clear from floor mosaics in Palestinian synagogues like Beth Shean (Plate XLVIII), and Ḥammath-Tiberias. There are also gold-leaf glasses where the curtain is seen behind the ark doors. The curtain was placed in front of the ark since the biblical ark had been placed "behind a *parokhet*" (Exodus 26:33). Medieval rabbinic sources refer to curtains in Ashkenazi synagogues, but no Torah ark curtain has survived from this period; the oldest extant curtain dates from 1592 and comes from Prague (Plate XXXIII). Many types of curtains are extant from the seventeenth century on, especially from German and Bohemian-Moravian synagogues (Plates XXXIII-XXXVIII). Some were made by skilled hands with complicated techniques and expensive materials; they were commissioned by

---

[12] Cf. J. Gutmann, "How Traditional are Our Traditions?" *Beauty in Holiness*, 417-19 and R. Mellinkoff, "The Round-Topped Tablets of the Law: Sacred Symbol and Emblem of Evil," *Journal of Jewish Art*, 1 (1974), 28-43.

prominent members of the community, or important societies or organizations to show their devotion and their social standing within the community. Such curtains often served as models for other curtains. Frequently they are lined with two columns and a rectangular centerpiece or mirror of expensive cloth much older than the curtain itself (Plates XXXIII-XXXIV). The upper part of such a curtain carried extensive votive inscriptions. Other curtains come from town workshops and were made in a series according to stencils. The donor in a curtain of this type simply had his name inscribed as an addition. There are also many curtains that were home made. These specimens of folk art have plain fabrics and use simple techniques. Brocade curtains with silver-gilt or gold thread and semi-precious stones with twisted columns and Jewish symbols and inscriptions over the entire surface of the curtain were also popular, especially in Germany where they were made by such professionals as Elkanah Naumburg and Jakob Koppel Gans (Plate XXXV). In Italy many curtains were embroidered by women (Plate XXXVI). While in Ashkenazi communities the curtains are usually hung outside the ark, in Sephardi and in Italian synagogues the curtain, when used, is placed behind the ark doors. Islamic communities like Bokhara would use two or more curtains—one outside the ark, one inside the ark, and one behind the Torah cases. In Italy on festive occasions like *Shavuot* and *Simḥat Torah*, it was customary in some communities to have lavish curtains showing Mount Sinai, the Ten Commandments, and the walled city of Jerusalem and its Temple. In Ashkenazi communities, special white curtains were at times used for the circumcision ceremony and bore the text of the ceremony (Plate XXXVIIb). White curtains were also used for *Yom Kippur* and *Rosh ha-Shanah*, green curtains for *Shavuot* and *Sukkot*. Some curtains with biblical scenes are known from Ashkenazi communities (Plate XXXVIII); the practice is already mentioned by the seventeenth-eighteenth-century Ashkenazi rabbi Ezekiel Katzenellenbogen. Joel Sirkes of sixteenth-seventeenth-century Poland also records the making of a curtain from the garment of a deceased wife. Many Bohemian-Moravian ark curtains also have bells attached to the top of the curtain.[13]

From the eighteenth century on, it became customary to hang a horizontal valance, called *kapporet*, above the ark curtain. These valances come predominantly from Germany and Bohemia. They usually had seven or five scallops and were donated, sometimes along with the curtain, sometimes separately (Plates XXXV, XXXIX). Often the *kapporet* has three crowns embroidered on it, a Hebrew inscription and two cherubim with outstretched wings hovering over the Decalogue (Exodus 25:20 and 37:9). On the scallops we often find such ritual Temple appurtenances as the efod, copper altar, menorah, table of showbread, copper laver and frontlet of pure gold.

The *ner tamid*, encountered in all synagogues, was not part of the standard synagogue equipment until the seventeenth century and is not mentioned in rabbinic sources before that time. The *ner tamid* was hung in front of and above the Torah ark and curtain, alluding thereby to the light set up "to burn regularly (*ner tamid*, Exodus 27:20 and Leviticus 24:2) outside the curtain."Many of these silver or brass eternal lights, in fact, closely resemble those hung in neighboring churches (Plate XLa). In the eighteenth

---

[13] Cf. F. Landsberger, "Old-Time Torah Curtains," *Beauty in Holiness*, 125-63; H. Volavková, *The Synagogue Treasures of Bohemia and Moravia* (Prague, 1949); D. Davidovitch, "A Rare Parokhet for the Circumcision Ceremony," *Museum Haaretz Yearbook*, 15-16 (1974), 112-18.

century, Wilhelm Christiani still spoke of simple eternal lights made of glass filled with olive oil and suspended from brass chains. In Eastern Europe, especially Poland, one finds mention of the placement of the eternal light in a cupboard or niche on the wall near the entrance to the synagogue. Whether a seven-branched menorah stood next to the Torah ark, as depicted in early synagogue mosaics, is not certain (Plate XLVIII). The seven-branched lampstand, however, served in many a medieval church to symbolize Christ and/ or the Virgin. In the medieval synagogue it became customary to maintain a menorah—one which unlike its Temple prototype was intended for the celebration of *Ḥanukkah* only and thus was fashioned with nine branches (eight plus a *shamash*, the "servant" light) (Plate XL). In Spanish synagogues the *Ḥanukkah* menorah stood in the center of the building. In Ashkenazi synagogues the Ḥanukkah menorah stood in the south or to the right of the Torah ark. Isaac Tyrnau of fourteenth-fifteenth-century Hungary (*Sefer Minhagim* 52b) writes: "One kindles the Ḥanukkah [light] in the south of the synagogue in memory of the Temple menorah that stood in the south."

Israel Isserlein (*Terumat ha-Deshen* 48a) of fifteenth-century Austria records: "We kindle Ḥanukkah [lights] in the synagogue towards the southern side as a memorial to the [Temple] menorah." This custom arose to "enable the ignorant to hear the blessings recited correctly . . ." (sixteenth-century Rabbi Mordecai Jaffe, *Levush, Oraḥ Ḥayyim, Hilkhot Ḥanukkah* 671:8) and "to spread the miracle in public" (thirteenth-century Lunel rabbi, Abraham ben Nathan Hayarḥi, *Sefer ha-Manhig* 105a). By the seventeenth-century these lampstands had begun to resemble the seven-branched Temple menorah, but were, of course, equipped with two additional branches for the required Ḥanukkah lights. Medieval Ashkenazi synagogues frequently included a ledge for candles. These candles were sometimes called *tamid* lights and were kindled after *Yom Kippur* in memory of the departed souls of one's father and mother.

These practices—calling the ark *aron ha-kodesh* (II Chronicles 35:3), inscribing the Decalogue on its inside doors (Exodus 25:16 and Deuteronomy 10:2), utilizing a *parokhet* (Exodus 26:33) and a *kapporet* (Exodus 25:20 and 37:9) to cover the ark, suspending a *ner tamid* (Exodus 27:20 and Leviticus 24:2) in front of it and placing a *Ḥanukkah menorah* (Exodus 26:35 and 40:24) on its south side—all arose in Ashkenazi Central European synagogues between the fourteenth and eighteenth centuries. Such practices attest to the fact that the synagogue was to the Ashkenazi Jew his surrogate Temple, his small sanctuary (*mikdash me'at*) in Exile. Praying in his *mikdash me'at* promised him that he would behold the messianic Temple of the future when all exiles would be resurrected in Jerusalem.

Many medieval synagogues had an antechamber (sometimes called *polisah* in Germany), which held locked cases (called *genizah*) for objects—torn prayer books or Torah scrolls—that were *pasul* (ritually unfit for use). A pewter or copper water dispenser (in Italy sometimes a marble basin) with handtowel was also found in the antechamber, so that the pious worshipper could wash his hands before praying. These water dispensers frequently carried the Hebrew inscription: "I wash my hands in innocence" (Psalms 26:6). Next to the entrance door stood a closed charity box (*kuppah shel tzedakah*) (Plate XLI). Sometimes the charity boxes were in the shape of an outstretched hand with a slot for donations. Charity is an important aspect of Judaism; making contributions was interpreted as showing concern for one's fellow human being before offering prayers. These charity boxes often bore the Hebrew inscription from Proverbs 21:14: "A gift in secret averts anger."

Next to the Torah ark, the most important synagogue furnishing was what is now called *bimah* (or *bimah shel etz* from the Greek word *bema* = platform). In Sephardi congregations it is usually referred to as a *tevah* or *migdal* (or *migdal etz*), while in medieval Ashkenazi synagogues it was called *almemor* (from Arabic *al-minbar*, the pulpit in the mosque) or *shulḥan*. In Ashkenazi congregations it was from the *bimah* that the Torah was read; in Sephardi congregations it was customary both to intone prayer and to read the Torah from the *bimah*. The *bimah* and the Torah ark were the most important liturgical furnishings and constantly vied with each other for prominence—was the container of the Torah to be emphasized or its recitation or should both be given equal stress? The *bimah* (*almemor*) dominated the medieval Ashkenazi synagogue. It occupied the center of the synagogue following the recommendation of Maimonides (*Yad, Hilkhot Tefillah* XI:3), and was usually a raised dais approached by steps; often a wrought iron fence complete with doors and benches encircled the *bimah* (Plate XLII). In Spain, a wooden tower (*migdal etz*) with parapet and ledge was raised on a wooden platform supported by columns and approached by a long, straight stairway, as we can see from medieval Spanish Hebrew miniatures. In Italian synagogues, both the Torah ark and the *bimah* had equal prominence and stood at opposite ends of the synagogue building harmoniously balancing each other (Plate XLIII). Sometimes the *bimah* was an elaborate marble structure approached by a curved double flight of steps. Later Sephardi synagogues in Holland and England featured a *bimah* (called *tevah*) which was a rectangular balustrated wood platform in the rear of the synagogue raised by a few steps and girt with benches (Plate I). In East European masonry and wooden synagogues, the most important liturgical component is again the *bimah*. The four pillars or columns set in the center of the synagogue helped emphasize the centrality of Torah reading; the four-vault support covered the *bimah* like a canopy. From the nineteenth century on, however, the Torah arks have been the most prominent element in the synagogue. Within these enclosures or platforms (known as *bimot*) stood a pulpit with a cover of silk or velvet, sometimes embroidered and sometimes bearing inscriptions (Plate XLIIb), and usually called *mappah* (it was also known as a *Machse Decke* in Germany). The pulpit in the Ashkenazi synagogue was frequently built like a cabinet which could be locked and which contained a *haftarah* scroll (a parchment scroll with prophetic readings) on two rollers and a cover, a *megillah* (scroll of Esther read on *Purim*), a *kiddush* beaker (for sanctification over wine on Sabbath and holidays), a *havdalah* candle and spice box (for the Sabbath separation ceremony), a black and white *shofar* (black for excommunication rites and white for *Rosh ha-Shanah* and *Yom Kippur*), and a *Schulklopfer* for the *shamash* (a knocker for the synagogue functionary, often called *Schammes*) to summon worshippers to the synagogue by knocking on their doors for daily prayers, though not on Sabbath.

Common in the Ashkenazi synagogue was also a lectern or stand to the right and below the *aron* (Torah ark) from which the cantor or reader of the prayer service would recite the daily liturgy. Called *amud* or *amod*, it, too, was frequently covered with a *mappah* (cloth), made of silk or velvet. In front of the *amud* was a *Sheviti* tablet, made of paper or brass, which usually carried the verse "I have set (*sheviti*) the Lord before me always" (Psalm 16:8); sometimes the *Sheviti* carried such decorations as Temple/Tabernacle implements, crowns, birds and lions. Meditating on the tablets' words was meant to help the cantor banish impure thoughts from his mind so that he could concentrate on prayer.

The role of women in the synagogue is most problematic. They do not seem to have had a special place set aside in the early or medieval synagogue. Eliezer ben Joel of thirteenth-century Rhineland still speaks of curtains pulled across the men's hall to accomodate women for Sabbath sermons. In the late Middle Ages, a so-called *Weiber Schule* (or *ezrat nashim*, "court of women")—an adjoining separate room—was added to the synagogue. Later we find galleries or balconies introduced for women. Nowadays, though the Orthodox synagogue continues to segregate women at worship, liberal synagogues seat men and women together in the main sanctuary.

Next to the Torah reading, prayer constitutes the most important element in the synagogue. Prayers were recited from prayer books, known as *maḥzor* (later *maḥzor* designated only the *Rosh ha-Shanah* and *Yom Kippur* liturgy) and *siddur* (for daily and Sabbath use). During morning (*shaharit*) prayers, the pious male Jews puts on a prayer shawl known as a *tallit* (Plate XLIV). Originally Jews dressed as people did in the Hellenistic and Roman worlds and simply wore a tunic and a cloak (known as *tallit*). Only the rectangular cloak (*tallit*) had fringes (*tzitzit*) attached to the four corners as symbols of God's commandments as stated in Numbers 15:37ff.: "Speak to the Israelite people and instruct them to make for themselves fringes on the corners of their garments throughout the generations. . . That shall be your fringe; look at it and recall the commandments of the Lord and observe them, so that you do not follow your heart and eyes in your lustful urge." Deuteronomy 22:12 reads: "You shall make tassels (*gedilim*) on the four corners of the garment with which you cover yourself." The *tallit* was an ordinary overgarment worn outdoors, not a special shawl, the wearing of which arose much later. During the Middle Ages, under the influence of *Kabbalah* (mysticism), the biblical commandments on the *tallit* were extended to include the 613 rabbinic commandments. This was done by ingenious *gematria* (number symbolism). The numerical value of the word *tzitzit* equals 600; the five knots and the eight ṣtrings of the *tzitzit* equals 13 thus totaling 613. The traditional prayer shawl (*tallit*) is now usually made of wool and is worn over the shoulders (sometimes over the head of the worshipper); it consists of four square corners (*kenafot*) through which a small round hole is made for the threads of the four *tzitzit* drawn through each side to make eight hanging strings. The eight strings are tied, wound and knotted so that they contain five knots and four sections—the part of the fringes that hangs loose below the last knot is called *gedilim* (tassels). In remembrance of the "thread of blue" (Numbers 15:38), *tallitot* have blue, or as is now more customary black, stripes woven into the white fabric. The *tallit* is frequently given as a wedding present by the bride or nowadays as a *Bar Mitzvah* gift. Wealthy Jews would have a richly embroidered silver or gold strip sewn onto the top of the upper border of the *tallit* known as *atarah* or *ateret* (crown). This strip of white rayon is sewn on the *tallit* in order to distinguish between the upper and the lower side of the *tallit* and to prevent the *tallit* from sliding down. When a man dies, he is buried in the *tallit* he wore during his lifetime, though the *tzitzit* are cut off to indicate that he is now exempt from performing the prescribed *mitzvot* (commandments).

The *tallit* is worn every day for morning prayer, whereas the *tefillin* are not worn during the morning services on Sabbath and holidays. Since the Middle Ages, every male Jew on reaching religious majority at age thirteen and a day has been expected to wear the *tallit* and *tefillin* during prayer. The *tallit* is donned first by the pious worshipper; then the *tefillin* or phylacteries, which consist of two black leather boxes (known as *batim*) with leather straps (*retzu'ot*) attached to them (Plate XLIV). The leather must come from a *kasher* (ritually slaughtered) animal. One of the boxes (*bayit*) is placed on the forehead and is called *tefillin shel rosh* (phylactery of the head) and the other is usually placed on the left arm opposite the heart and called *tefillin shel yad* (phylactery of the hand); left-handed persons will place it on the right arm. Wearing the *tefillin* next to the heart and opposite the brain is meant to intimate, according to tradition, that the mind and all the senses ought to be subject to God's service. The *tefillin shel yad* is put on first; it contains a single strip of parchment on which four biblical passages are inscribed (Exodus 13:1-10; 13:11-16; Deuteronomy 6:4-9; 11:13-21). The *tefillin shel rosh* contains four compartments, but the same four biblical passages are written on four separate pieces of parchment and are placed separately in each compartment—each is tied with a strand of calf's hair and the aperture into which the parchment is inserted is closed with a square piece of thick leather (called *titora*). This box has two letters *shin*, one on the outside right hand side, the other on the left side. One *shin* on the right is in the regular shape of the letter; the other has four strokes instead of three. The two straps attached to the back of the *tefillin shel rosh* must be black on the outside and hang loosely in front of the wearer. The leather strap of the *tefillin shel yad* is wound around the forearm seven times between elbow and wrist and the remaining part of the strap is wrapped around the hands' middle finger in a prescribed manner. The Ashkenazim usually wind the strap counter-clockwise; the Sephardim clockwise. Many reasons are given for this arrangement. Under the influence of *Kabbalah*, the arrangement of the *tefillin* was interpreted as spelling out the word *Shaddai* (Almighty) and hence plays an important role in the *tefillin* ritual. When the straps are wound around the arm and hand, they are so arranged as to form the Hebrew letter *shin*. The top part of the three windings around the middle finger take on the shape of the Hebrew letter *daled* and the underpart of the strap around the middle finger is tied to form a *yud*. Together they again make up the word *Shaddai*. Another interpretation has it that the letter *shin* is embossed on the head box, while the knot of the head straps at the nape of the neck is in the shape of a *daled* and the *yud* is formed by the straps that pass through the hand phylactery. Thus again the shin on the head box and the letters formed by the knots of the two straps make up the word *Shaddai*. The rite of wearing *tefillin* can only be traced back to the rabbinic period; the time and place of its origin are lost. The earliest known phylacteries come from the Qumran caves and may date from the first century C.E. During this early period, they were probably part of everyday dress and were not worn just for prayer. They were apparently removed during work, at night and when entering a place defined as ritually impure. In addition to the prescribed texts they once included the text of the Decalogue. Tradition links *tefillin*—a word not found in the Bible—with the enigmatic *totafot* of the Bible: "You shall bind them as a sign on your hand and let them serve as a symbol (*totafot*, usually translated as frontlets) on your forehead" (literally: "between your eyes", Exodus 13:16 and Deuteronomy 6:8 and 11:18). The only ceremonial objects linked with the phylacteries are special *tefillin* cases of incised silver dating from the eighteenth century and later.

An important prayer ceremony recited on major holidays in the synagogue (in Israel the rite is performed daily) is the priestly benediction. During the repetition of the final benedictions of the *Shemoneh Esreh* (18 benedictions, a significant prayer also known as *Amidah* because it is recited standing) in the *musaf* (additional) service, the *kohanim*

(men of priestly descent) present at services leave the congregation to take off their shoes
and have their hands washed by the Levites present. For this purpose, special silver or
pewter utensils are used (Plates XLVI-XLVII). This *minhag* (custom) is a reminder of
the Temple ritual when the priests had their hands and feet washed by the Levites at the
conclusion of the daily sacrificial service before blessing the people. The *kohanim* return
barefoot (as Moses was commanded to remove his shoes for he was standing on holy ground
when Divinity appeared to him—in Exodus 3:5—and one was not permitted to enter
the Temple Mount with shoes on) and take their place in front of the Torah ark on a so-
called *dukhan* (platform) or area designated for the priestly blessing (*birkat kohanim*, the
ceremony is also called *duchaning* or *duchanen*. The three-fold blessings are recited during
the ceremonial, as recorded in Numbers 6:23-27. The *kohanim* cover their hands and faces
with a *tallit* and raise their hands so that the thumbs rest in the corner of the eyes towards
the nose. The index fingers are brought together to form a triangle—a reference to the
three-fold blessing or the three-fold division of Jewry—and a V space is left between
the two outer and the two inner fingers (Plates IIb, XLV, XLVI). The congregation is
enjoined not to look at the *kohanim*, for the glare of the *Shekhinah* (Divine presence)
resting upon their hands, it was believed, could cause blindness.

Symbols play no insignificant role in the synagogue. Probably the oldest Jewish symbol
is the *menorah*—the seven-branched lampstand which, according to Exodus 25:31-40
and 37:17-24, once stood in the wilderness Tabernacle. Many scholars agree that these
elaborate descriptions in Exodus stem from the priestly writers of the fifth century
B.C.E., who were explaining the cult and its objects as they actually existed in the Second
Temple, but had hardly been present in the Tabernacle during the wilderness wanderings.
The priests projected the menorah back into the wilderness period in order to give it
Mosaic sanction, a lofty antiquity, and to legitimize a new object and practice in the
Temple cult of the fifth century B.C.E. We know that no menorah stood in the Shilo
Temple or in the Tent which David erected in Jerusalem. Even the ten *menorot* (I Kings
7:49 and Jeremiah 52:19) Solomon placed in his Temple are not identical in shape or
form with the menorah that ostensibly stood in the wilderness Tabernacle. Both Josephus
and the rabbis were bothered by this obvious biblical contradiction and tried to resolve it.
Josephus in his *Antiquities* (VIII. 3:7) implied that Solomon made 10,000 lampstands,
according to the command of Moses, one of which he dedicated to the Temple. The rabbis
(Babylonian Talmud, *Menaḥot* 98b) intimated that the menorah of Moses stood in the
middle of the Temple with five lampstands to the right and five lampstands to the left
of it. Yet the Bible gives no warrant for such a conclusion. That the menorah was not a
fiction is borne out by its prominent depiction on the Arch of Titus in Rome; it was clearly
one of the spoils of the sacked and burned Jerusalem Temple in 70 C.E. It is also described
earlier in the *Book of Maccabees* (I Maccabees 1:21). The menorah projected back into the
book of Exodus was in all likelihood *the* menorah which had stood in the Second Jerusalem
Temple and which the Romans took as booty to Rome. The confusion between the ten
historical menorot of Solomon's Temple and the ahistorical menorot in the wilderness
Tabernacle stems from the efforts of the priestly writers to legitimize the menorah that
existed in the Second Temple. The meaning of this biblical menorah is not too clear;

some scholars feel that its symbolism is rooted in the sacred cosmic almond tree of ancient Near Eastern mythology.[14]

The menorah continued to play a prominent role in early synagogue and catacomb decorations, but its meaning and function in this new context are obscure (Plate III, XLVIII). The synagogue and catacomb depictions usually show a menorah with a three legged base whereas the Temple menorah represented on the Arch of Titus and on coins issued by King Antigonus rests on a solid base. The evidence, however, is problematic and insufficient for any solid conclusions as to the form of the base of the Temple menorah. Therefore, arguments that the synagogue and catacomb menorot do not resemble the Temple menorah, since the reproduction of the Temple menorah is forbidden in the Babylonian Talmud (*Menahot* 28b, *Rosh ha-Shanah* 24a, *Avodah Zarah* 43a) have little validity. Moreover, it is frequently overlooked that these menorah images come from areas under the jurisdiction of the Palestinian Talmud, which has no such prohibition. When the Palestinian Talmud ceased to have legal, binding power in the early Middle Ages and the Babylonian Talmud became normative for all Jewish communities, the reproduction of the Temple menorah in the synagogue was indeed banned. It is only in the nineteenth century that the seven-branched menorah reappears—and then not in a traditionalist context, but in the Reform synagogue (or temple), which did not accept the authority of the Babylonian Talmud's proscription (reechoed in the *Shulḥan Arukh, Yoreh De'ah* 141:8) and also denied the concept that the synagogue is a surrogate for the Temple. The Reformers, in furnishing their houses of worship with replicas of the seven-branched menorah, were asserting that the synagogue was the Temple here and now; there was no need to pray and hope for the restoration of *the* Temple in messianic times.

The early synagogue and Jewish catacombs made use of many pagan symbols such as eagles, birds, erotes, victories, mythological figures, lions, centaurs, and sirens, but these depictions are unlikely to have retained anything of their original symbolic value; they served a strictly decorative purpose.[15] In Jewish catacomb and synagogue paintings and mosaics dating from the third to the sixth century, two menorot are usually found flanking a Torah ark along with a *lulav* and *etrog*, a shofar, and what has been identified as an incense shovel (Plates III, XLVIII). These images appear programmatic and must have significance, yet no definite conclusions can be reached as to what that significance was.

It is true that all of these symbols were known to the Temple cult; since the synagogue served as a substitute Temple, these synagogue symbols or implements may simply have been a reminder of the lost Temple cult. Some scholars, however, see in the Torah ark a symbolic portal which guaranteed the worshipper dedicated to the Law ultimate entrance to the dwelling place of divinity. One could also interpret these symbols as undergirding the synagogue's claim to be the rightful successor to the Temple. The ancient Temple ark is now the container of *Torah*—God's entire revelation both biblical and rabbinic, the Oral and the Written Law—and is surrounded by the newly interpreted rabbinic symbols. Thus, for instance, the *lulav* and *etrog* refer now to the synagogal celebration of *Sukkot*; the ram's horn (*shofar*) is symbolic of the synagogal holiday of *Rosh ha-Shanah* when God,

---

[14] Cf. J. Gutmann "A Note on the Temple Menorah," Gutmann, *No Graven Images*, 36-38 and L. Yarden, *The Tree of Light: A Study of the Menorah* (Ithaca, 1971).
[15] Cf. M. Smith, "Goodenough's *Jewish Symbols* in Retrospect," Gutmann, *The Synagogue*, 194-209.

according to the rabbis, remembers the *akedah* (the Sacrifice of Abraham) and accounts it to Israel's credit for the forgiveness of its sins. As the two-fold Law, the *Torah*, according to the rabbis, had been handed down on *Shavuot*, perhaps the Torah ark, the container of God's entire revelation, also symbolizes the celebration of *Shavuot*. The *maḥtah*, the incense shovel, is difficult to interpret. It was linked in the Temple with *Yom Kippur*, (Leviticus 16), when the high priest entered the Holy of Holies with an incense shovel yet no such ceremony is described for the synagogue. Although the identification of the incense shovel is generally accepted, others see in this depiction a snuff-shovel, an incense burner, a charity box, a lectern or even a *magrepha*. Again the meaning of the two menorot on either side of the Torah ark yields no ready answers. We are not certain whether bronze menorot actually stood next to the Torah ark, singly or in pairs, though there is some literary and archaeological evidence which would make the above a distinct possibility. If the other symbols can be linked with synagogal holidays and celebrations, did the seven-branched lampstand perhaps also symbolize a significant synagogal holiday, such as the Sabbath? Extant literary sources make no such association of linking the seven-branched lampstand with the seventh day of rest (*Shabbat*), so that the above interpretation is simply a working hypothesis.

The medieval synagogue avoids the seven-branched lampstand and closely follows the proscriptions of the Babylonian Talmud against fashioning a seven-branched Temple menorah for synagogal use. Instead, the practice arose of placing a nine-branched menorah next to the Torah ark and associating it with the celebration of Ḥanukkah (Plate XL). The meaning of the ancient synagogue menorah has not been deciphered and many theories have been propounded. It has been explained as a messianic, pietistic, cosmic, eschatological mystic and national symbol. The latter is understandable in the light of the adoption of the *Magen David* for the national flag of Israel and the menorah as the emblem of the new state of Israel. The menorah may have had eschatological or cosmic significance. As a cosmic symbol it may be the image of God or may represent the heavens or the cosmos; its lights are sometimes equated in extant literature with the planets and the *Shekhinah*. It may also be an eschatological symbol of salvation as it appears within the *clipeus* of Jewish sarcophagi, where the wish is expressed that the righteous dead within the wreath of divine life (the immortal circle of God) be elevated to the stars and achieve ultimate victory over death.

Among the few symbols found in medieval synagogues are three crowns, frequently encountered, and standing for Torah, priesthood, and kingship. *Pirkei Avot* (*Ethics of the Fathers*) 4:13 had clearly stated: "R. Simeon said: There are three crowns—the crown of the Law (Torah), the crown of Priesthood and the crown of Kingship, but the crown of a good name exceeds them all." (Plate XXXIXb). A ewer or pitcher and hands spread in blessing are also encountered (Plates XXXVIIa, XLVI). The spread hands refer to the priestly benediction and are symbolic of priestly lineage; the pitcher was used by the Levites to wash the hands of the priests and is therefore a symbol of Levitical extraction. Often we find the lion—symbol of the tribe of Judah, for as Genesis 49:9 has it, "Judah is a lion's whelp." The lion also symbolized royalty as King David, the messianic king, is linked with the house of Judah.

The two tablets with the Ten Commandments symbolize the transmission of divine legislation (*Torah*) to Moses at Sinai. The depictions of leopards, eagles, gazelles and lions refer to the *Pirkei Avot* 5:20, where Judah ben Tema is quoted: "Be strong as the leopard and swift as the eagle, fleet as the gazelle and brave as the lion to do the will of your Father who is in heaven."

As late as the nineteenth century, Rabbi Isaac Elḥanan Spektor, of Kovno, Lithuania, warned the local Reform congregation to remove the *Magen David* ("Shield of David") which graced the roof of their house of worship. Spektor's attitude seems strange today when the *Magen David* serves most Jewish houses of worship—traditionalist as well as liberal—as a symbol of Judaism. Already in the late eighteenth century in Western Europe the Magen David was coming into popular use, perhaps as a meaningful new sign which could express or symbolize Judaism. It appears at that time on Jewish ceremonial objects, on synagogue buildings and seals. The twentieth century has seen the use of the symbol reinforced by two major factors. 1. In 1897, at Basel, Switzerland, the Magen David was officially adopted as the symbol of the new movement established to promote political Zionism (since 1948, the Magen David has been on the official flag of Israel). 2. In the 1930's and 40's the Nazis forced all Jews in their lands to wear a badge of shame—the yellow Magen David with the word *Jude* (Jew) emblazoned on it.

These two experiences of twentieth-century Jews have made what had long been a neutral sign into one of the holiest symbols of Judaism, simultaneously embodying pride in the reborn state of Israel and a recollection of the Holocaust.

The Magen David is a hexagram or six-pointed star. It appears as early as the Bronze Age and is at home in cultures and civilizations widely removed in time and geographic area. Mesopotamia, India, Greece, and Etruria are among the places where it has been found—but without any discoverable meaning. Possibly it was an ornament or had magical connotations. Only occasionally before the 1890's is it found in a Jewish context; the oldest Jewish example is from seventh-century B.C.E. Sidon, a seal belonging to one Joshua ben Asayahu. In the synagogue at Capernaum, Galilee, a synagogue which may date from the fourth century C.E., the Magen David is found alongside the pentagram and the swastika, but there is no reason to assume that the Magen David or the other signs on the synagogue stone frieze served any but decorative purposes.

In the Middle Ages, the Magen David appears quite frequently in the decorations of European and Islamic Hebrew manuscripts and even on some synagogues, but appears to have no distinct Jewish symbolic connotation; it is also found on the seals of the Christian kings of Navarre, on mediaeval church objects, and on cathedrals. As a matter of fact, what is today called Magen David was generally known as the Seal of Solomon in the Middle Ages, especially in Jewish, Christian and Islamic magical texts. In the medieval Islamic world the hexagram was popular and was widely used. Generally known, especially in Arab sources, as the Seal of Solomon, it gradually became linked with a magic ring or seal believed to give King Solomon control over demons. An early Jewish source in the Babylonian Talmud (*Gittin* 68a-b) already mentions it.

The hexagram and pentagram, it should be pointed out, both carried the designation "Seal of Solomon" and were employed in both Christianity and Islam as symbols with magical or amuletic power. On the parchment of many medieval *mezuzot* (capsules placed on the doorposts of every Jewish home) the hexagram and pentagram (Seal of Solomon) were written out and also served as a talisman or had magical powers to ward off evil spirits.

In addition to being called "Seal of Solomon", the Magen David was also linked in medieval Jewish sources with a protective shield bearing the seventy-two holy names of God and that of the angel Taftatiyyah (also called Metatron). Amulets in the shape of a hexagram with the word Taftatiyyah on it are known; after 1500, the name *Shaddai* (Almighty) was frequently substituted for that of the angel. Other medieval sources, however, attach the designation Shield of David to Psalm 67 written out in the shape of the seven-branched menorah. Accordingly, it was believed that David's battle shield had been engraved with the text of Psalm 67 in the form of a menorah. No clear picture of the Magen David develops, as the hexagram shape could apparently be called either Magen David or Seal of Solomon. Two unrelated historic events greatly contributed to the emergence of the Magen David, the hexagram, as a distinct Jewish symbol in the nineteenth century. In 1354 when King Charles IV granted the Prague Jewish community the privilege of having its own flag, a hexagram appeared on the banner; later documents refer to it as King David's flag. Thus in Prague, Bohemia, the Magen David began to assume a semi-official, politico-religious function as a distinct Jewish symbol. Its use in Prague was widespread; it is found as a seal in Prague's printed Hebrew books and on tombstones and Jewish ceremonial objects. It is from Prague that the hexagram, Magen David, moved to other Jewish communities like Vienna, Amsterdam and Moravia.

In the seventeenth century, the followers of the messianic pretender Shabbetai Zevi, also adopted the Magen David; for them it was a messianic symbol of redemption. Amulets of the movement bore the hexagram with the Hebrew letters *MBD* (*meshiah ben David*, Messiah, son of David). Thus the shield of David came to be the shield of the son of David, the hoped-for Messiah.[16]

---

[16] Cf. G. Scholem, "Magen David," *Encyclopaedia Judaica* (1971), XI, 687-97.

CATALOGUE OF ILLUSTRATIONS

Plate I

Raising and Exposing the Torah Scroll, Amsterdam, 1725. Engraving by Bernard Picart. From A. Rubens, *A Jewish Iconography*, London, 1981, p. 44, No. 442. Rubens Collection, London.

Plate IIa

The Torah Scribe. Etching by Moses Ephraim Lilien, Germany, ca. 1910. From L. Brieger, *E. M. Lilien. Eine künstlerische Entwicklung um die Jahrhundertwende*. Berlin-Wien, 1922, p. 8 and J. Gutmann, *Jerusalem by Ephraim Moses Lilien*, New York, 1976, p. 97.

Plate IIb

Torah Scroll, Ark, Binder, Mantle of the Law, Priestly Benediction. Erlang, 1748. Etching by G. Eichler from plates to J. C. G. Bodenschatz's *Kirchliche Verfassung*. Rubens, p. 56, No. 590. Rubens Collection, London.

Plate III a-b

Jewish Gold Glasses. Jewish catacombs, Rome, first half of fourth century. Open Torah arks flanked by lions, *menorah*, *lulav*, *etrog* and *shofar*. Inscription: "Drink, so you may live." K. Weitzmann, ed., *Age of Spirituality*, New York, 1979, pp. 380-81; K. Katz, P. P. Kahane, M. Broshi, *From the Beginning*, New York, 1968, p. 118, fig. 103. Jerusalem, Israel Museum.

Plate IV

Biblical Figure (identified as Ezra, Moses, etc. ?). Dura-Europos Synagogue Mural, Syria, 244-45. National Museum, Damascus. From E. R. Goodenough, *Jewish Symbols in the Greco-Roman Period*, XI, New York, 1964, fig. 326.

Plate Va

Torah Case. Kaifeng, China, late seventeenth century (?). Wood case, gilt and lacquered in red. Similar case in the Royal Ontario Museum, Toronto, Canada, 931.18.1. W. C. White, *Chinese Jews, a Compilation of Matters Relating to the Jews of K'aifeng*, Toronto, 1942, II, pp. 28-29, plates 7-8; M. Pollak, *Mandarins, Jews and Missionaries: The Jewish Experience in the Chinese Empire*, Philadelphia, 1980, p. 208, fig. 20. Hebrew Union College Skirball Museum, Los Angeles, No. 57.2. Photo: Bob Lopez.

Plate Vb

Torah Case with *Rimmonim*. Aleppo, Syria, 1710. Artist: Joseph Laḥam. Prismatic wood case overlaid with eight silver plaques. A. Dothan, "On the History of the Ancient Synagogue in Aleppo," *Sefunot*, 1 (1956), 25-61 (Hebrew). Present whereabouts unknown.

Plate VIa

Torah Case with *Rimmonim*. Nablus, Palestine, 1756. Silver repoussée, coral and semi-precious stones. Inscription: "The Holy Congregation of Shekhem in the year corresponding to 1756." J. Gutmann, *Jewish Ceremonial Art*, New York, 1964, fig. 9. Hebrew Union College Skirball Museum, Los Angeles, No. 57.1. Photo: Marvin Rand.

Plate VIb

Torah Case with *Rimmonim*. Iraq, 1897. Wood case overlaid with silver, parcel-gilt. Inscription: "This case was consecrated by Ezra Enzarut in memory of his mother." *The Maurice Spertus Museum of Judaica. An Illustrated Catalog of Selected Objects*, Chicago, 1974, p. 10. Spertus Museum, Chicago.

Plate VIIa

Binder for *Sefer Torah*. Padua, Italy, 1572. Linen with embroidered borders and inscriptions: "Praised be the One who in His holiness has given the Torah to His people Israel. The righteous flourish like the palm tree (Psalms 92:13), declares Tamar, the wife of Moses. I will pay my vows to the Lord, in the year 5332 (= 1572)." Italian Synagogue, Jerusalem. From U. Nahon, *Holy Arks and Ritual Appurtenances from Italy in Israel*, Tel Aviv, 1970 (Hebrew and English), p. 150.

Plate VIIb

Binder for *Sefer Torah (Wimpel)*. Germany, June 27, 1844. Linen, painted. Inscription: "Joseph, son of Jonah, born on Thursday, the tenth of *Tammuz*, 5604 (= June 27, 1844). The zodiacal sign is cancer. *Spertus Museum Catalog*, p. 22 Spertus Museum, Chicago.

Plate VIIIa

Torah Mantle. Saarlois, France, 1747. Red velvet, relief embroidery with metallic thread. On the twisted columns the Dream of Jacob is depicted. On top, heraldic lions carry a crown. Inscription: "Crown of Torah 5507 (= 1747), Leiser and his wife, Keile." Cf. the similar curtain, plate XXXVIII. N. Rosenan, *L'année juive. Vue à travers l'exposition du Musée Juif de Suisse à Bâle*, Zürich, 1976, p. 65, No. 1. Jüdisches Museum der Schweiz, Basel, No. JMS/72. Photo: Thomas Hartmann.

Plate VIIIb

Torah Mantle. Germany, 18th century. Rose velvet border, gold fringe and gold woven braid. At bottom is a well, flanked by two columns, each topped by a gold medallion appliqué containing a red rampant lion. Top, a crown with brass ring and inscription: "Crown of Torah." Hebrew Union College Skirball Museum, No. 60.10

Plate IX

Torah Mantle. Gibraltar, 1764. Crimson silk velvet embroidered on gold and silver thread. Four panels—Aaron, the priest with ephod, censer and miter. Inscription: "Crown of Priesthood." Moses carries a Scroll with the words: "This is the Law which Moses placed before the Children of Israel (Deuteronomy 4:44)." Above Moses: "Crown of Torah." Not visible are two additional panels with inscriptions: "Crown of Royalty" and "The Crown of a good name excells them all (Ethics of the Fathers 4:17)." and the name of the donor (?): "Solomon Abraham, 5524 (= 1764)." Jewish Museum, London, *Catalogue*, No. 67, p. 19, plate XLVI.

Plate Xa-b

Torah Mantle. Holland, early 18th century. Mantle of brocade on red silk ground. Three upright orphreys of red velvet, embroidered in gold and silver thread in high relief. The Tablets of the Ten Commandments, inscribed in Hebrew, are shown between twisted columns. The table of showbread and an open Torah ark are also depicted. The designs are taken from Daniel Marot's book of engraved patterns. Spanish and Portuguese Synagogue, London. R. D. Barnett, ed., *Treasures of a London Temple*, London, 1951, p. 59, plates VIII-IX.

Plate XI

Torah Mantle. Miniature from Rothschild *Siddur*, Florence, Italy, 1492. An Italian Jew, wrapped in a *Tallit*, holds the Torah scroll with its mantle. He stands next to the Hebrew blessing recited before the reading of the Torah: *"There is none like You, O Lord, among the gods that are worshipped."* B. Narkiss, *Hebrew Illuminated Manuscripts*, Jerusalem, 1969, p. 144. Jewish Theological Seminary of America Library, New York, folio 125v.

Plate XIIa

Torah Shield. Amsterdam, 1610. Silver. Made for Jacob Tirado by an Amsterdam silversmith from Emden (?). Inscription: "For the New Moonsdays." Portuguese Synagogue, Amsterdam. M. H. Gans, ed., *Memorbook. History of Dutch Jewry from the Renaissance to 1940*, Baarn, 1977, p. 30. From F. Landsberger, "The Origin of European Torah Decorations," *Beauty in Holiness*, ed. J. Gutmann, p. 105.

Plate XIIb

Torah Shield. Strasbourg, ca. 1660. Master: Daniel Hammerer. Silver-gilt. Inscriptions: On the center plaque is the word "Sukkot." Around the center: "Jacob, son of Asher Segal (i.e. Levi) of Ulsheim (? Ulsenheim, W. Bavaria)." On the reverse: "Jabit, daughter of blessed memory, in the year 5442 (= 1682)." The Jewish Museum, London, *Catalogue*, No. 136, pp. 30-31, plate LXIV.

Plate XIIIa

Torah Shield. Augsburg, ca. 1700. Silver-gilt. Master: Michael Mayer (?). Inscription on plaque: "Holy Sabbath." Oval outline chased with arms supporting crown; twisted columns on side. The Jewish Museum, London, *Catalogue*, No. 139, p. 32, plate LXIV.

Plate XIIIb

Torah Shield. Augsburg, 1773-75. Silver-gilt. Master: Samuel Bardet (?). Inscription on plaque: "Passover." Above engraved Tablets of the Law with Hebrew Decalogue is an inscription: "And Isaac went out to meditate in the field (Genesis 24:63)" and the chronogram for 5536 (= 1776). Below two hands emerging from clouds are holding roses. The Jewish Museum, London, *Catalogue*, No. 143, p. 33, plate LXIII.

Plate XIV

Torah Shield. Augsburg, 1803 (?). Silver-gilt. Master: Bizel. Inscription on plaque: "Yom Kippur." Above the plaque are the inscribed tablets of the Ten Commandments and the *menorah* (the seven-branched lampstand). The inscription in the garlanded circle reads: "Belongs to Jacob, son of Jacob Lipmann Hechingen and his wife Rebecca, 5585 (=1825)." Formerly Feinberg Collection, Detroit, *Exhibition of Jewish Ceremonial Art, The Detroit Institute of Arts*, Detroit, 1951, p. 20, No. 61. Now Jerusalem, Israel Museum, No. 54.68. Y. Cohen, "Torah Breastplates from Augsburg in the Israel Museum," *Israel Museum News*, 14 (1978), 83.

Plate XVa

Torah Shield. Nuremberg, ca. 1700. Silver-gilt. Inscription on plaque: "Sabbath." On top are two rampant lions next to a crown. Above the crown is the double-headed eagle of the Holy Roman Empire. At the bottom are two running unicorns. A similar Torah shield is in the Jewish Museum, New York, F 3686. F. Landsberger, "A German Torah Ornamentation," *Beauty in Holiness*, p. 115, fig. 6; Gutmann, *Jewish Ceremonial Art*, plate III. Hebrew Union College Skirball Museum, No. 7.21. Photo: Marvin Rand.

Plate XVb

Torah Shield. Poland, early 19th century. Silver-gilt. Inscription on plaque: "Passover." Two rampant lions upholding coronet. In center a Torah ark with doors is flanked by two columns. Beneath columns are two small running stags. Hebrew Union College Skirball Museum, Los Angeles, No. 7.17. Photo: Marvin Rand.

Plate XVI

Torah Shield and *Rimmonim*. Munich, 1828. Silver-gilt with semi-precious stones. Master: Georg Zeiller. Inscription on plaque: "Passover." Swagged cartouche below with inset silver oval has the Hebrew inscription, "Belonging to Asher ben Naphtali Niedermeier of Thalmessing, 1858." Landsberger, "A German Torah Ornamentation," *Beauty in Holiness*, p. 108, fig. 1. Hebrew Union College Skirball Museum, Los Angeles, Nos. 7.5 and 47.11.

Plate XVII

Torah Shield. Italy, 18th century. Silver. Inscription in upper cartouche, "First Torah Scroll." Formerly in Modena, Italy synagogue, now in the Italian synagogue in Jerusalem, Israel. From U. Nahon, *Holy Arks and Ritual Appurtenances from Italy in Israel*, Tel Aviv, 1970, p. 167.

Plate XVIIIa

Torah Pointer. Switzerland (?), 18th century. Silver. Inscription: "The president Moses, son of Joseph (Guggenheim) and his wife Teichle, daughter of Eliakum of Lengnau have donated this pointer (*yad*) in honor of God and the Torah in the year 5505 (= 1745)." Rosenan, *L'année juive*, p. 70, fig. 59. Jüdisches Museum der Schweiz, Basel, No. JMS/80. Photo: Thomas Hartmann.

Plate XVIIIb

Torah Pointer. S. Germany, 19th century. Wood. Inscription: "Moses is truth and his Torah is truth." Rosenan, *L'année juive*, p. 70, fig. 60. Jüdisches Museum der Schweiz, Basel, No. JMS/81. Photo: Thomas Hartmann.

Plate XVIIIc

Torah Pointer. Germany, 18th century. Silver. Hebrew Union College Skirball Museum, Los Angeles, No. 44.27. Photo: Erich Hockley.

Plate XIX

Rimmon. Sicily, 15th century. Silver filigree with semi-precious stones. Inscriptions from Psalms 19:8-10: "The Law of the Lord" [is perfect reviving the soul]; "the testimony of the Lord," [is sure making wise the simple]; "the precepts of the Lord," [are right, rejoicing the heart]; "the commandment of the Lord" [is pure, enlightening the eyes]; "the fear of the Lord" [is clean, enduring forever]; "the ordinances of the Lord" [are true and righteous altogether]. "These *rimmonim* are holy to the Lord. In the synagogue of the Jews of Cammarata, the Lord protect it, Amen." Cathedral Treasury of Palma de Mallorca, Spain. F. Cantera-J. M.ª Millas, *Las inscripciones hebraicas de España*, Madrid, 1956, pp. 389-93; G. Llompart, "La fecha y circumstancias del arribo de 'las rimmonim' de la catedral de Mallorca," *Sefarad*, 30 (1970), 48-51. From Gutmann, *Jewish Ceremonial Art*, fig. 1.

Plate XX

Rimmonim. Frankfurt-am-Main, Germany, early 18th century, Silver. Master: Jeremias Zobel. Tower form with two open hexagonal tiers with open work crown and bells. F. Landsberger, "A German Torah Ornamentation," *Beauty in Holiness*, p. 112, fig. 4; Gutmann, *Jewish Ceremonial Art*, fig. 3. Hebrew Union College Skirball Museum, Los Angeles, No. 47.24.

Plate XXIa

Rimmonim. Augsburg, 1757-59. Silver-gilt. Master: C.B. Openwork bodies; the bells hang from lion masks. Crown finial supported by rampant lions holding oval plaques with Hebrew inscriptions. The Jewish Museum, London, *Catalogue*, No. 123, p. 28, plate LV.

Plate XXIb

Rimmonim. Rotterdam, 1783. Silver. Master: I.B. Hexagonal two-tiered turret form with gilt crown and bells. The Jewish Museum, London, *Catalogue*, No. 126, p. 29, plate LIV.

Plate XXII

Rimmonim. London, England, 1724. Silver. Master: Abraham de Oliveyra. Hexagonal three-tiered bulbous cupola form, topped by crown and flaming vase finial. The Jewish Museum, London, *Catalogue*, No. 114, p. 27, plate LXI.

Plate XXIII

Rimmonim. New York, ca. 1765. Silver-gilt. Master: Myer Myers. Three-tiered cupola form, topped by crown and pineapple finial. Touro Synagogue, Newport, Rhode Island. G. Schoenberger, "The Ritual Silver made by Myer Myers," *Beauty in Holiness*, p. 70, fig. 3; J. W. Rosenbaum, *Myer Myers, Goldsmith, 1723-1795*, Philadelphia, 1954, p. 99 and p. 67, plate 1.

Plate XXIVa

Rimmonim and Crown. Padua, Italy, 18th century. Silver-gilt. Hebrew inscription around band of crown has the date 1862. Shell scrolls, flower-filled urns, and cartouches with such Jewish symbols as the *menorah* and the tablets of the Law. *Rimmonim* have hexagonal three-tiered turret form and terminate in a flower-filled urn. Below six bells and pomegranates pendant on long chains. Temple Israel, West Bloomfield, Michigan.

Exhibition of Jewish Ceremonial Art, Detroit, Institute of Fine Arts, Detroit, 1951, p. 14, figs. 37-39.

Plate XXIVb

Rimmonim. Leghorn (?), Italy, late 17th century. Silver. Hexagonal two-tiered turret form with vases, flowers and flower finials. Six bells pendant on long chains. The Jewish Museum, London, *Catalogue*, No. 105, p. 26, plate LVI.

Plate XXV

Torah Crown for *Simḥat Torah*. Alsace (?), mid-19th century. Cardboard with silk ribbons, textile leaves and flowers. Rosenan, *L'année juive*, p. 68, fig. 40. Jüdisches Museum der Schweiz, Basel, No. JMS/91. Photo: Thomas Hartmann.

Plate XXVI

Torah Crown. S. Germany, late 18th century. Silver-gilt. Continuous Hebrew inscription around bottom band: "Belonging to Koppel ben Ḥanokh and his wife Edel (?), daughter of R. Nathan of Burgkundstadt. May your children (?) be raised for the Torah, for the marriage canopy and for good deeds. May Judah rejoice in you, 1770/71." Upper band has within the repoussée ovals the signs of zodiac. Rampant lions holds oval finial on top of a large gilt sphere. Gutmann, *Jewish Ceremonial Art*, fig. 6. Hebrew Union College Skirball Museum, Los Angeles, No. 58.11.

Plate XXVIIa

Torah Crown. Amsterdam, early 18th century. Silver. Master: Pieter van Hoven. Portuguese inscription underneath crown: "Consecrated by Eliao de M. Crasto on the occasion of his having been honored as *Ḥatan Bereshit* in the year 5472 (= 1711)."

Plate XXVIIb

Torah Crown with *Rimmonim*. Amsterdam, 1714 (?). Silver. Master: Pieter van Hoven (?). Portuguese inscription on underside of crown: "In memory of Mordecai Hizkiyahu Namias de Crasto on the day of his death, 13 Iyyar 5476 (= 5 May, 1716), who did sacred service for the holy congregation of Mikve Israel." Both crowns are from Mikve Israel-Emanuel Synagogue, Curaçao, Netherlands, Antilles. I. S. and S. H. Emmanuel, *History of the Jews of the Netherlands Antilles*, Cincinnati, 1970, I, p. 249, fig. 69 and II, p. 575, fig. 220. Photo: Fischer.

Plate XXVIIIa

Torah Crown. Galicia, early 19th century. Silver-gilt. Circular open work crown composed of six rampant lions, alternating doves supporting a canopy banded by a Hebrew inscription: "Crown of Torah, Crown of Priesthood, Crown of Kingdom, 1819." The whole is surmounted by a tier with six stags carrying a dome with floral top. Formerly Feinberg Collection, Detroit; present location unknown. *Exhibition of Jewish Ceremonial Art*, Detroit, 1951, p. 14, No. 31. Cf. the crown in the Jewish Museum, New York, *Danzig, 1939*, Catalogue, p. 96, No. 77.

Plate XXVIIIb

Torah Crown, Poland, ca. 1815. Silver. Circlet of crown has figure of Moses with tablets, Aaron wearing high priestly garments, David holding a model of the Temple (?), Solomon playing the harp (?), Jacob sleeping while angels ascend the ladder and Abraham with Isaac about to be sacrificed. Canopy suported by rampant lions, filigree crown finial with dove. All figures are identified by Hebrew inscriptions. The inscription on the lower rim reads: "This crown belongs to Yeḥezkiel, son of Isaac, his wife Mameni, daughter of Meir, his grandson Isaac Meir, his grandson Samuel Isaac. 'This is my handiwork in which I glory' (Isaiah 60:21), Dov, son of Yehuda Katz (i.e. Cohen); Tzevi, son of Israel; Eliezer, son of David, 5573 (= 1813)." The Jewish Museum, London, *Catalogue*, p. 30, No. 135, plate LXI and color plate 4.

Plate XXIXa

Torah Crown, North Italy, 1797. Red bronze. Hebrew inscription: "Completed on the eve of the holiday of the giving of the Torah (*Shavuot*) in the year 5557 (= 1797). For the Torah portion and of Zebulun he said: 'Rejoice, O Zebulun, on your journeys' (Deuteronomy 33:18); 'a crown of glory and a diadem of glory' (Isaiah 28:5); for the honor of the Torah 'drawn up in full and secured' (II Samuel 23:5)." Open cylinder form with intertwining bands forming cartouches which contain a censer and the miter of the high priest; two symbols are missing. Hebrew Union College Skirball Museum, Los Angeles, No. 58.4. Photo: Erich Hockley.

Plate XXIXb

Torah Crown. North Italy, 18th century. Silver-gilt. Open cylinder form with fruit, flowers, sea-shell motifs and *menorah*. Gutmann, *Jewish Ceremonial Art*. Color plate I. Hebrew Union College Skirball Museum, No. 58.12.

Plate XXXa

Simḥat Torah. Amsterdam, Portuguese Synagogue, 1675. Engraved by Bernard Picart, ca. 1725. Rubens, p. 45, No. 449. Rubens Collection, London.

Plate XXXb

Hekhal (Torah Ark). Amsterdam, Portuguese Synagogue, 1675. R. Wischnitzer, *The Architecture of the European Synagogue*, Philadelphia, 1964, pp. 90ff. J. F. van Agt, *Synagogen in Amsterdam*, 's-Gravenhage, 1974, p. 47, fig. 40.

Plate XXXIa

Torah Ark with Ten Commandments. Mantua-Sermide Synagogue, 1543, now in Jerusalem, Italian Synagogue. Wood. From Nahon, *Holy Arks and Ritual Appurtenances in Israel*, p. 51.

Plate XXXIb

Torah Ark with Ten Commandments. Pesaro Synagogue, 1646, now in Jerusalem, Italian Synagogue. Wood, Decalogue painted on interior of ark doors. From Nahon, *Holy Arks*, p. 106.

Plate XXXIIa-b

Miniature Torah Ark. Vienna, Austria, 1783. Silver-gilt. Architectural form in two tiers resting on four lions. In the center are the inscribed Hebrew Tablets of the Law; below, on a scroll, is the Hebrew inscription: "I keep the Lord before me always (Psalms 16:8)."

Behind the closed double doors the Tabernacle is revealed with Aaron, the high priest, and Moses with the Decalogue. Hebrew Union College Skirball Museum, Los Angeles, No. 30.2. Photo: Erich Hockley.

Plate XXXIII

Torah Ark Curtain. Prague, Bohemia, 1592 for the Altneu Synagogue. Velvet with colored silk appliqué. The middle section's checkerboard pattern with red, green and purple roses is flanked by two pillars. Center inscription: "Solomon [and his wife] Golda [Perlsticker]." Above is a crown, underneath which is the Hebrew inscription: "Crown of Torah." The inscription surrounding the crown reads: "Solomon, son of Abraham, called Perlsticker, in the year 350 (=1590)." The inscription in the right lozenge: "Pinḥas, son of Solomon Perlsticker, in the year 352 (= 1592)." The inscription in the left lozenge: "Gautel, daughter of R. Judah Cohen, in the year 352 (= 1592)." Solomon and his son Pinḥas were probably the embroiderers of this curtain. The inscriptions in the upper section are taken from I Kings 5:26, Exodus 35:32, 35. Prague, The State Jewish Museum, Inv. No. 27.365. O Herbenová, "Synagogenvorhänge des 17. Jahrhunderts aus Böhmen und Mähren," *Waffen- und Kostümkunde*, 10 (1968), pp. 107ff., fig. 1. From O. Muneles, ed., *Prague Ghetto in the Renaissance Period*, Prague, 1965, pp. 105-06, figs. 56-57.

Plate XXXIVa

Torah Ark Curtain. Bohemia, 1697. Satin, velvet with metallic appliqué. The central panel is red satin and the top panel is tan velvet. The inscription reads: "This is a gift of the esteemed Löb, son of Ḥenokh Schick and his wife Malka, daughter of Zalman Küdarsch (?), in the year 5457 (= 1697)." Cf. a similar curtain in H. Volavková, *The Synagogue Treasures of Bohemia and Moravia*, Prague, 1949, fig. 9, p. 29. Hebrew Union College Skirball Museum, No. 59.41.

Plate XXXIVb

Torah Ark Curtain. Prague, Bohemia, 1623. Grossenhof Synagogue, later Altneu Synagogue. Centerpiece of gold-red brocade is from Italy, 16th century. The borders are dark-red velvet with gold and silver embroidery. Above the columns is the inscription: "Crown of Torah"; "Gift of Jacob, son of Abraham Bassewi and his wife Hendel, daughter of Eberl Gronim." The chronogram over the words "for a festive occasion" is 383 (= 1623). Prague, The State Jewish Museum, Inv. No. 27.396. From Volavková, *The Synagogue Treasures*, p. 30, figs. 16-19.

Plate XXXV

Torah Ark Curtain and Valance. Bavaria, 1727 (?). Embroidered by Jakob Koppel Gans. Velvet with appliqué embroidery. Last at Krumbach Synagogue in Germany; probably destroyed. The inscription on the valance: "I have set the Lord always before me (Psalms 16:8)" and "Know before whom you are standing (Babylonian Talmud, *Berakhot* 28b)." Below are the "Crowns of Torah, Priesthood and Kingdom." The implements of the Tabernacle depicted on the valance scallops are: the Decalogue, the laver and its stand, the *menorah*, the copper altar and the table of showbread. The inscription on the curtain: "This is the blessing with which God blessed Moses. Made by Jakob Koppel, son of [Judah ?] Löb Gans, Goldsticker from Höchstadt." The donor of the curtain and valance was Löb, son of Abraham from Kriegshaber and his wife Hendel,daughter of Nathan Segal. Cf. a similar curtain in The Jewish Museum, New York, F 1285a-b. From F. Landsberger, "Old Time Torah Curtains," *Beauty in Holiness*, pp. 156-57 and 137, fig. 9.

Plate XXXVIa

Torah Ark Curtain. Italy, 17th century. Azure brocade and flowers with Tablets of the Law embroidered in gold. Synagogue in Rome, now in Jerusalem, Italian Synagogue. From Nahon, *Holy Arks*, p. 137.

Plate XXXVIb

Torah Ark Curtain. Italy, 18th century. Brocade embroidered with gold and colored threads. Synagogue in Modena, now in Jerusalem, Italian Synagogue. Donated in memory of Mordecai Angelo Donati. From Nahon, *Holy Arks*, p. 140.

Plate XXXVIIa

Torah Ark Curtain. Frankfurt-am-Main, Germany, 1730. White satin inset center panel with embroidery; wine-red satin border. Top panel has a crown in the center flanked by two rampant lions. Beneath crown are the blessing hands of the priest and over the crown is the inscription "Crown of Priesthood." "This is the gift of Moses, son of Jakob Katz (i.e. Cohen), Frankfurt-am-Main, in the year of deliverance;" chronogram corresponding to 5490 (= 1730) "and his wife Tauberl (i.e. dove), daughter of Israel Isserl, Frankfurt-am-Oder." L. S. Freehof and B. King, *Embroideries and Fabrics for Synagogue and Home*, New York, 1966, p. 58, fig. 28. Hebrew Union College Skirball Museum, No. 59.37.

Plate XXXVIIb

Torah Ark Curtain for the Circumcision Ceremony. Germany, 1715. Blue satin, leather appliqué, silk embroidery. Between urns, a large crown and inscription: "Crown of Torah. Made for the Gabbai of charitable funds, the officer Leiser Heidelberg, may he be blessed;" chronogram corresponding to 5475 (= 1715). Then follows the standard text of the circumcision ceremony, beginning with the blessing over wine and ending with the blessing: "As he entered into the covenant [of Abraham], so may he be raised for the study of Torah, for the wedding canopy and for good deeds." Cf. Jewish Museum, *Danzig, 1939* Catalogue, Nos. 6, 138 (D 250, 257), and D. Davidovitch, "A Rare Parokhet for the Circumcision Ceremony," *Museum Haaretz Yearbook*, 15-16 (1974), 112-18. Hebrew Union College Skirball Museum, Los Angeles, No. 59.40.

Plate XXXVIII

Torah Ark Curtain. Saarlois, France, 1740. Velvet with damask border and metallic thread. The centerpiece has the prophet Zechariah being awakened by an angel. Below is the vision of the *menorah*, which is flanked by the olive trees (Zechariah 4). The *menorah* has the Hebrew inscription: "lampstand of Zechariah". Next to the angel is a drawn bow with the inscription: "Constellation *keshet* (= bow or Sagittarius)." The Hebrew inscription above and below the centerpiece reads: "Crown of Torah—Abraham (?). This is the curtain donated by Feibel, son of Sender and his wife Rebecca, daughter of Feibush Worms of

Saarlois, in the year 5500 (=1740)." Cf. the Torah mantle, plate VIIIa. Formerly in the Randolph Hearst collection; present whereabouts unknown.

Plate XXXIXa

Kapporet. Germany, 1714. Maroon velvet with metallic embroidery. "The Crown of Torah" is flanked by two cherubim wings. Inscription to the right and left of wings: "And the cherubim shall have their wings spread out above, shielding the cover with their wings (Exodus 25:20)." Inscription below crown and wings: "The Holy Burial Society made this gift;" chronogram corresponding to 5474 (= 1714). Below are five curved scallops with "the golden *menorah*, the table of showbread, the two tablets" of the Ten Commandments. The inscription between the Tabernacle implements is from Psalm 16:8 and Babylonian Talmud, *Berakhot* 28b. Freehof-King, *Embroideries*, p. 72, fig. 35. Hebrew Union College Skirball Museum, Los Angeles, No. 59.39.

Plate XXXIb

Kapporet. Prague, Bohemia, 1724. Beige damask, silver and gold embroidery and relief appliqué, with two side wings and seven scallops. Upper panel contains three crowns; the center one is supported by two emblematic eagles with displayed wings and entitled: "the two cherubim." The inscription underneath the wings reads: "This is the gift of the pious women seated in the upper women's section (*ezrat nashim*) of the High Synagogue and embroidered by Meile (?) for the glory of God and the *Shekhinah* (= Divine Presence)." Chronogram corresponding to 5484 (= 1724). The scallops contain the frontlet of pure gold, the table of showbread, the laver and its stand, the Ark with the Ten Commandments, the golden incense altar, the golden *menorah* and the High Priest's breastpiece. Similar *kapporot* in the Jewish Museum, New York, S 1 and the State Jewish Museum, Prague. Hebrew Union College Skirball Museum, Los Angeles, No. 59.59.

Plate XLa

Synagogue *Menorah* for *Ḥanukkah.* Germany, 1655-56. Bronze. Formerly in the Synagogue of Worms, destroyed in 1938. Inscription: "A gift from the president [of the congregation], Issachar, son of Moses David Gans." Chronogram 5416 (= 1655-56). O. Böcher, "Die Alte Synagoge zu Worms," *Festschrift zur Wiedereinweihung der Alten Synagoge zu Worms*, ed. E. Roth, Frankfurt/Main, 1961, p. 86, p. 114, fig. 5.

Plate XLb

Synagogue *Menorah* for *Ḥanukkah.* Germany, early 18th century. Bronze. Formerly in synagogue of Aschaffenburg, Bavaria. Hebrew inscription: "This *menorah* is a gift for the house of worship from Pessel (?), the wife of Elkanah, of blessed memory, Aschaffenburg, 5466 (= 1705-06)." F. Landsberger, "Old Hanukkah Lamps," *Beauty in Holiness*, p. 307f. Hebrew Union College Skirball Museum, No. 27.73. Photo: Allan Walker.

Plate XLI

Charity Money Box. Poland, 17th century. Formerly in the Stara (Old) Synagogue of Kazimierz, Cracow, Poland. Destroyed by the Nazis and rebuilt in 1959. Inscription: "A gift in secret averts anger (Proverbs 21:14)" and "The throne is established in righteousness (Proverbs 16:12)." R. Wischnitzer, *The Architecture of the European Synagogue*,

Philadelphia, 1964, p. 55ff. *Stara Bóżnica Kazimierska, Muzeum Historyczne M. Krakowa,* n. d., fig. 9.

Plate XLIIa

Bimah (Almemor) of Synagogue of Worms. Worms, Germany, 1620. Stone. Watercolor by Heinrich Hoffmann, ca. 1840. Destroyed in 1938, rebuilt in 1961. Wischnitzer, *Architecture of the European Synagogue,* pp. 48-49; Böcher, "Alte Synagoge zu Worms," p. 79ff. and 50-52.

Plate XLIIb

Bimah (Almemor) of Synagogue of Kazimierz, Cracow, Poland. Poland, 15th century (?). Late Gothic wrought iron grill. Destroyed by Nazis and rebuilt in 1959. Wischnitzer, *Architecture of the European Synagogue,* pp. 54ff.; *Stara Bóżnica Kazimierska,* fig. 7.

Plate XLIIIa

Torah Ark of Scuola Grande Tedesca. Venice, Italy, 17th century. Wood-gilt. Inscription: "Gift of the eldest of the Zemel brothers, Menaḥem Cividale, son of Joseph, triumphant and victorious is he (Zechariah 9:9), in the year 5432 (= 1672)." Other Hebrew inscriptions are taken from Psalms 107:32 and II Samuel 23:8.

Plate XLIIIb

Bimah of the Scuola Grande Tedesca. Venice, Italy, 17th century. Wood-gilt. Wischnitzer, *The Architecture of the European Synagogue,* pp. 63ff.; *Jewish Art Treasures in Venice,* New York, n. d., pp. 23-24, 50.

Plate XLIVa

Tallit and Phylacteries and a Jew wearing them. Amsterdam, 1725. Engraving by Bernard Picart. From Rubens, p. 44, No. 439. Rubens Collection, London.

Plate XLIVb

Tallit and Phylacteries. Erlang, Germany, 1748. Etching from plates of J. C. G. Bodenschatz, *Kirchliche Verfassung.* From Rubens, p. 58, No. 602. Rubens Collection, London.

Plate XLV

The Priestly Benediction in the Portuguese Synagogue at The Hague. Amsterdam, ca. 1725. Engraving by Bernard Picart. From Rubens, p. 44, No. 441. Rubens Collection, London.

Plate XLVIa-b

Levitical Set to Wash the Hands of the *Kohanim* (Priests). Amsterdam, 1748 (?). Laver and Ewer. Silver. Master: Gerrit Boberhot. Ewer and laver have a design of the spread blessing hands of the priests. The laver has a Portuguese inscription: "Gift of Abigail Nunes [Redondo] (?)." Mikve Israel-Emmanuel Synagogue, Curaçao, Netherlands Antilles. Emmanuel, *History of the Jews of the Netherlands Antilles,* I, p. 240, fig. 56. Photo: Fischer.

Plate XLVII

Levitical Set to Wash the Hands of the *Kohanim* (Priests). London, 1768. Laver and

Ewer. Silver. Master: Abraham Portal. Inscription: "New Synagogue Leadenhall Street." The Jewish Museum, London, *Catalogue*, No. 192, p. 38, plate LXXI.

Plate XLVIII

Torah Ark with Curtain and Jewish Symbols. Beth Shean Synagogue Floor Mosaic, Palestine, sixth century. Katz, Kahane, Broshi, *From the Beginning*, color plate, pp. 116-17; Weitzmann, *Age of Spirituality*, pp. 375-76. Photo: D. Harris.

PLATES

Plate I

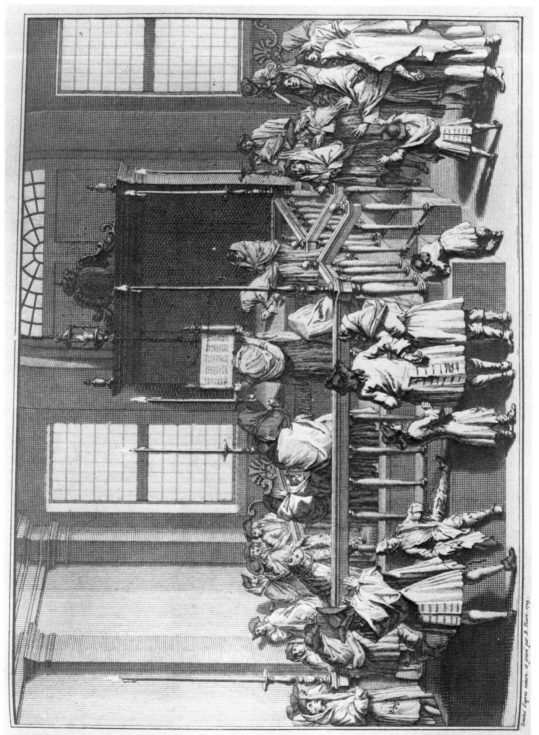

Raising and Exposing the Torah Scroll

Plate II

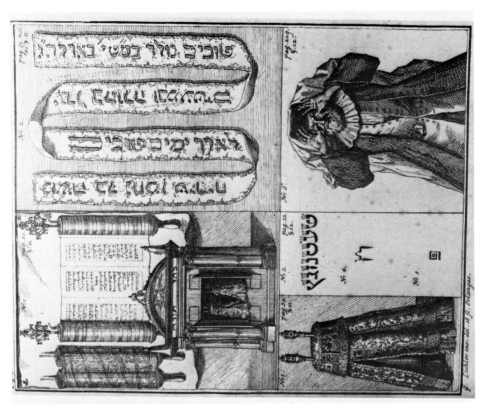

Torah Vestments, Priestly Benediction

b

Torah Scribe

a

Plate III

a

b   Jewish Gold Glasses

Plate IV

Biblical Figure. Dura-Europos Synagogue Mural

Plate V

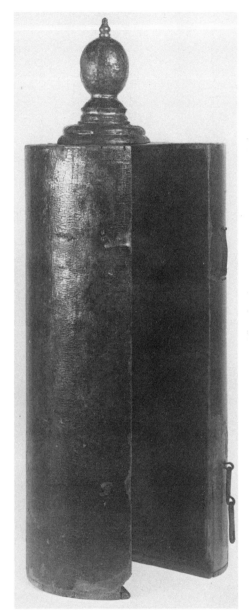

a   Torah Case   Torah Case with *Rimmonim*   b

Plate VI

a   Torah Cases with *Rimmonim*   b

Plate VII

b

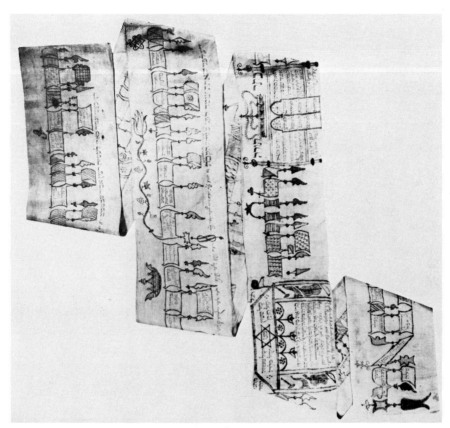

Binder for *Sefer Torah* (*Wimpel*)

a

Binder for *Sefer Torah*

Plate VIII

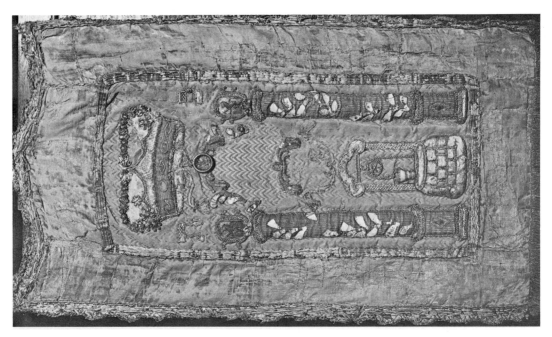

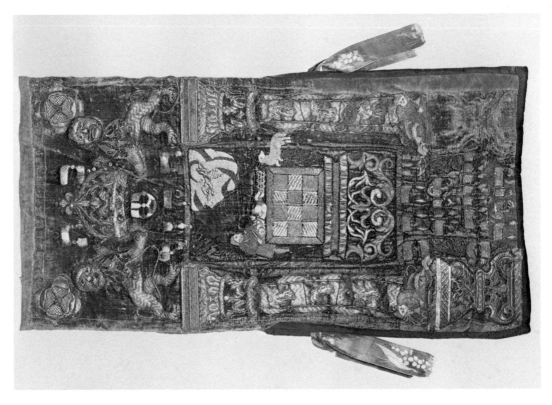

Torah Mantles

b

a

Plate IX

Torah Mantle

Plate X

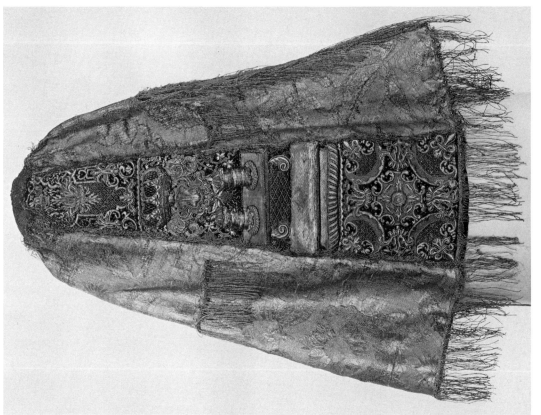

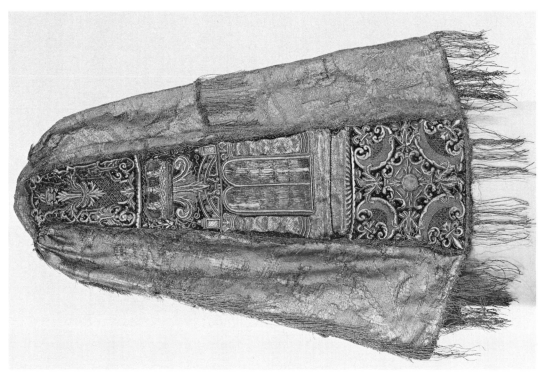

Torah Mantle

b

a

Plate XI

Torah Mantle

Plate XII

a

b   Torah Shields

Plate XIII

b

Torah Shields

a

Plate XIV

Torah Shield

Plate XV

a   Torah Shields   b

Plate XVI

Torah Shield and *Rimmonim*

Plate XVII

Torah Shield

Plate XVIII

a

b

c

Torah Pointers

Plate XIX

Rimmon

Plate XX

Rimmonim

Plate XXI

b

Rimmonim

a

Plate XXII

Rimmonim

Plate XXIII

Rimmonim

Plate XXIV

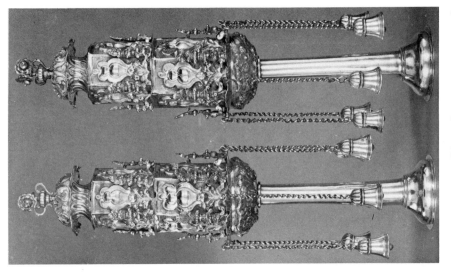

Rimmonim

Rimmonim and Torah Crown

Plate XXV

Torah Crown for *Simḥat Torah*

Plate XXVI

Torah Crown

Plate XXVII

a   Torah Crown

b   Torah Crown with *Rimmonim*

Plate XXVIII

b

a

Plate XXIX

a

b   Torah Crowns

Plate XXX

a   *Simḥat Torah*

b   *Hekhal* (Torah Ark)

Plate XXXI

a

b   Torah Arks with Ten Commandments

Plate XXXII

b

a

Miniature Torah Ark

Plate XXXIII

Torah Ark Curtain

Plate XXXIV

Torah Ark Curtains

b

a

Plate XXXV

Torah Ark Curtain and Valance

Plate XXXVI

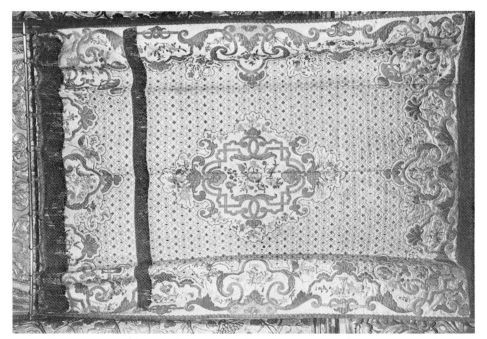

Torah Ark Curtains

b

a

Plate XXXVII

Torah Ark Curtain for the Circumcision Ceremony

b

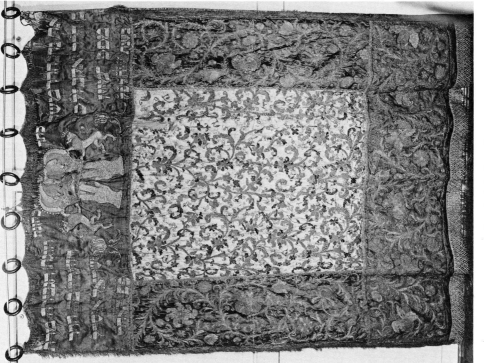

Torah Ark Curtain

a

Plate XXXVIII

Torah Ark Curtain

Plate XXXIX

a

b   *Kapporet*

Plate XL

a

b   Synagogue *Menorah* for *Ḥanukkah*

Plate XLI

Charity Money Box

Plate XLII

Bimah

b

a

Plate XLIII

Torah Ark

Bimah

Plate XLIV

b *Tallit* and Phylacteries

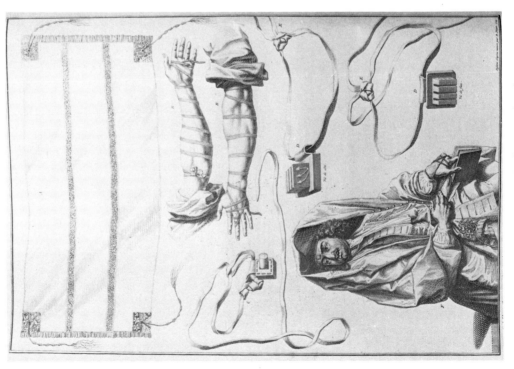

a *Tallit* and Phylacteries and a Jew wearing them

Plate XLV

Synagogue des Juifs Portugais à la Haye.

The Priestly Benediction

Plate XLVI

a

b   Levitical Set to Wash the Hands of the *Kohanim* (Priests)

Plate XLVII

Levitical Set to Wash the Hands of the *Kohanim* (Priests)

Plate XLVIII

Torah Ark with Curtain and Jewish Symbols